A HANDBOOK
of Grammar, Rhetoric, Mechanics, and Usage

A HANDBOOK

of Grammar, Rhetoric, Mechanics, and Usage

Newman P. Birk
and Genevieve B. Birk

The Bobbs-Merrill Company, Inc.
Indianapolis

Copyright © 1949, 1951, 1958, 1965 by The Odyssey Press.
Copyright © 1972 by The Bobbs-Merrill Company, Inc.
Printed in the United States of America
All rights reserved. No part of this book shall be
reproduced or transmitted in any form or by any means,
electronic or mechanical, including photocopying, recording,
or by any information or retrieval system, without written
permission from the Publisher:

       The Bobbs-Merrill Company, Inc.
       4300 West 62nd Street
       Indianapolis, Indiana 46268

Fifth Edition
Fifth Printing—1976
Library of Congress Catalog Card Number: 71-179751
ISBN 0-672-63275-6 (pbk)

INTRODUCTORY NOTE

This handbook is essentially Part Three of Birk and Birk, *Understanding and Using English,* Fifth Edition. It is printed as a separate volume at the request of teachers who want their students to have a basic guide to conventions of grammar, rhetoric, mechanics, and usage, but who are reluctant to ask students to buy the longer combined rhetoric and handbook. References to early chapters of *Understanding and Using English* have been deleted for this edition of the handbook; otherwise, the material is the same as in Part Three of the larger text.

Earlier versions of the handbook have been used differently in different classes. Sometimes teachers assign whole sections for review; exercises accompanying many of the articles make it possible to spend some time in class on problems of, for instance, punctuation, if a class needs this kind of review. Often teachers simply ask students to use the handbook for reference in writing and correcting papers. Articles are self-contained, with occasional references to other articles in which terms are defined; the student who has difficulty with agreement of pronouns, for example, can read the article on agreement without reading preceding material. For the student who has few technical difficulties in writing, the handbook may serve to clarify his instructor's comments on matters like emphasis, interest, and tone.

CONTENTS

Section 1. CONVENTIONS AND MEANING — 1

Section 2. SENTENCE ELEMENTS AND THEIR RELATIONSHIPS — 4

1. NOUNS: PLURALS AND POSSESSIVES 4
2. PRONOUNS: CLASSES AND CASE 7
3. PRONOUNS: AGREEMENT 10
4. PRONOUNS: REFERENCE 12
5. VERBS: PRINCIPAL PARTS 15
6. VERBS AND COMPLEMENTS 18
7. VERBS AND VERBALS 20
8. VERBS: AGREEMENT 23
9. VERBS: VOICE AND MOOD 27
10. VERBS: TENSE 29
11. ADJECTIVES AND ADVERBS 33
12. CONNECTIVES 36
13. PHRASES AND CLAUSES 40
14. FRAGMENTARY AND INCOMPLETE SENTENCES 42
15. FUSED AND RUN-TOGETHER SENTENCES 45
16. MODIFIERS 48
17. FAULTY RELATIONSHIPS OF SENTENCE ELEMENTS 51

Section 3. STYLE AND RHETORIC: SUMMARY AND REVIEW — 56

18. CHOICE OF WORDS 56
19. COHERENCE 57
20. CONCRETENESS 58
21. ECONOMY 59
22. EMPHASIS 59
23. FIGURATIVE LANGUAGE 60
24. GOOD PARAGRAPHS 62
25. INTEREST 62
26. LEVELS OF USAGE 63
27. PARALLELISM 63

28. REPETITION 64
29. SUBORDINATION 64
30. TONE 65
31. TRANSITIONS 66
32. UNITY AND FOCUS 66
33. VARIETY 67

Section 4. PUNCTUATION   69

34. APOSTROPHE 69
35. BRACKETS 71
36. COLON 71
37. COMMA 72
38. DASH 79
39. ELLIPSIS 80
40. EXCLAMATION POINT 80
41. HYPHEN 81
42. ITALICS 82
43. PARENTHESES 83
44. PERIOD 84
45. QUESTION MARKS 86
46. QUOTATION MARKS 87
47. QUOTATION MARKS WITH OTHER MARKS OF PUNCTUATION 88
48. SEMICOLON 90

Section 5. MECHANICS   92

49. SPELLING 92
50. CAPITALIZATION 104
51. TITLES 107
52. SYLLABIFICATION 108
53. NUMBERS 108
54. ABBREVIATIONS 109
55. MANUSCRIPT FORM 111
56. OUTLINE FORM 111

Section 6. USING THE DICTIONARY   118

Section 7. A GLOSSARY OF USAGE   124

Section 8. A NOTE ON PLAGIARISM   141

INDEX   144

CORRECTION SYMBOLS   150

HANDBOOK

Section 1

CONVENTIONS AND MEANING

Without conventions, the communication of meaning through words would be impossible. A word is a symbol that stands for and refers to an object, idea, or attitude; its basic meaning (what it refers to) is fixed by the customary use or convention of the language to which it belongs. If a writer, unclear about the meanings of words, says that he believes in "immorality" when he means *immortality,* or if he characterizes someone as "ingenious" when he means *ingenuous,* he fails to communicate; or, at best, he calls upon his reader to guess at the meaning intended but misstated. A convention is literally a "coming together." A speaker or writer and his audience are enabled to "come together" in understanding, to share experience and ideas, by their common acceptance of the conventional meanings of words.

Just as good English involves a knowledge of the established or agreed-upon meanings of words, it involves also—if the writer is at all concerned with the impression he will make on an informed audience—a knowledge of certain commonly accepted matters of usage. Most of this Handbook is concerned with these conventions of usage. Sometimes they are vital to the clear communication of meaning; when, as is often the case, they are not, an awareness of them is still important in much the same way that an awareness of other widely followed customs is important.

We live, of course, in times of rapid change—in attitudes, in dress, and in language; many once-established conventions are no longer observed; others may be thought to represent a stifling conformity. The wise nonconformist, however, understands the use of convention; when he chooses to depart from it, he does so purposefully and on principle, not unintentionally and blunderingly.

Some of the conventions of language, like many social conventions, are relatively unimportant matters of form, the observance of which depends on circumstances: a conventional rule for the use of the comma, for example, may be comparable to the conventional rule of speaking to strangers only after an introduction; neither the comma nor the introduction may be necessary. Other conventions, both of manners and of language, have a greater practical usefulness because they establish procedures which it is convenient to have established. For example, traditional good manners require a man to allow a woman to precede him through the door he has opened; having this practice established by convention is useful: it saves confusion and indecision at doors. Similarly, in language, certain uniform practices in capitalization, punctuation, and spelling are convenient for writers and readers: the writer is saved the trouble of working out his own system, and the reader is spared the greater trouble of adjusting to the personal eccentricities of each author. A writer may have good reason to take liberties with some of these conventional practices, just as a man may with good reason precede a woman through a door; but unless the reason is clear, he may appear to be discourteous and uninformed.

Still other conventions of manners and of language are so deeply rooted in custom or principle that one who violates them is likely to be considered ignorant or boorish by people trained in the conventions. The host who invites a guest to dinner and fails to provide a chair for him at the table violates a basic principle of hospitality; the writer who, through a comparable confusion of numbers, uses singular verbs with plural subjects violates a similarly basic principle of grammar. The person invited to eat the dinner or to read the book is justifiably annoyed; his impression of the host or of the writer is an unfavorable one.

This unfavorable impression brings us to the heart of the relationship between conventions and meaning. Ordinarily, the failure to observe conventions of language like those just mentioned does not interfere seriously with the factual part of meaning. The person who talks with his mouth full of food usually can be understood; but his listeners are not likely to be favorably impressed by what he is saying or to hope that he will continue his discourse. In a similar way, though a reader may be temporarily confused by misleading punctuation, by misplaced modifiers, or by vague pronoun reference, he can usually arrive at the factual meaning of the passage in spite of these obstacles. He will, however, feel an irritated disrespect for the writer who makes his communication needlessly difficult and will be offended by the writer's apparent attitude of discourtesy and disregard for his reader. Under these circumstances, the writer's intention will almost certainly be defeated: a reader is not easily persuaded or convinced by one with whom he is irritated, nor is he likely to trust the information of a writer who seems imprecise or incompetent. Understanding the conventions and scrutinizing one's writing to be sure that no careless violations have crept in will not, in themselves, produce positively successful writing. They will, though, free the writer from awkward and misleading expression, and from the adverse criticism of his readers.

In discussing the conventions of grammar, usage, and mechanics, we have tried to take into account the flexibility of language, and to indicate where usage is divided, how usage may differ in formal and informal situations, and what freedom the writer has in following or departing from certain conventions. As the student applies the conventions to his own writing, he should, of course, be further guided by his instructor's standards of correctness and appropriateness.

HANDBOOK

Section 2

SENTENCE ELEMENTS AND THEIR RELATIONSHIPS

1. NOUNS: PLURALS AND POSSESSIVES

A noun is traditionally defined as a word or group of words used to name a person, place, or thing. Nouns function in sentences as subjects, objects, and complements[1] of verbs or verbals, as appositives, as objects of prepositions, and as modifiers.

>*Subject: Tom* is here.
>*Direct object:* She bought the *books.*
>*Indirect object:* She gave her *mother* the money.
>*Complement:* George is her *husband.* He left, slamming the *door.*
>*Appositive:* Mr. Thompson, the acting *chairman,* called the meeting to order.
>*Object of a preposition:* He stood on the *corner.*
>*Modifier: Henry's* departure was well-timed.

Nouns show a change in form (i.e., are inflected) in the possessive case and, usually, when they change number.

[1] For a discussion of complements, see page 18.

Plurals of Nouns

a. **The plurals of nouns are generally formed by adding *s* or *es* to the singular.** The letter *s* forms the plural when it can be added to the singular and pronounced without adding a syllable (*bath, baths; cat, cats*); the letters *es* form the plural when the singular ends in a sound (*s, ch, sh, z, x*) that cannot unite with *s* to form one syllable.

Among the exceptions to this rule are: (1) unchanging plurals (*deer, deer; Japanese, Japanese*); (2) *en* plurals (*child, children*); (3) *f* to *v* plurals (*thief, thieves*); (4) some foreign plurals (*alumnus, alumni*); (5) plurals in which vowels change (*man, men; foot, feet*); (6) plurals formed with *es* even though the noun does not end with *s, ch, sh, z,* or *x* (*Negro, Negroes*). If you are uncertain about how a particular word forms its plural, look it up in the dictionary.

b. **Plurals of figures and letters are generally formed by adding an apostrophe plus *s*. *S* alone may be used if the apostrophe is not needed for clarity.**

dotted both i's; pronounce s's clearly; three size 7's; IOUs

Possessive Case

a. **Singular and plural nouns not ending in *s* or *z* add an apostrophe plus *s*.**

the child's toy; children's toys; the woman's hat; the women's hats

b. **Plural nouns ending in *s* or *z* add only an apostrophe.**

the Smiths' house; ladies' clothes; babies' bottles

c. **Singular nouns ending in *s* or *z* may add the apostrophe plus *s* or the apostrophe only.**

Keats' poetry or Keats's poetry

d. **To indicate joint or separate ownership, possessives are used as follows:**

(1) When two or more people are mentioned as owning an object in common, only the last of the names is given possessive form:

Mary and John's records show their taste for symphonic music.

(2) When two or more people are mentioned as owning separate objects, each name is given possessive form:

Ted's and Marshall's books are still in our attic. [I.e., Ted's books and Marshall's books are still in our attic.]

e. **When possession is attributed to inanimate objects, the *of* phrase may be preferable to the possessive case form.**

the shoulder of the road [rather than the road's shoulder]

Usage is divided, however, and some of the numerous exceptions to this generalization are such common phrases as *a day's journey, a week's wages, a stone's throw, an hour's delay, the sun's rays, the earth's circumference, an arm's length.*

f. Possessive with the gerund.[2] **Nouns serving as modifiers of gerunds are usually given the possessive form, particularly in written English.**

We were all surprised by Eliot's refusing to go. [*Refusing*, a gerund, is modified by the possessive *Eliot's*.]

In colloquial usage, the noun modifying a gerund is often not given the possessive form.

EXERCISES

I. In the sentences below, point out the single nouns and the groups of words which function as nouns. What is the function in the sentence of each noun or noun construction?

1. That Tom was lazy was clear to his sisters.
2. Martha sold Jack a paper.
3. The boys know where they intend to go.
4. Alice is the president's wife.
5. To break the rule is to be suspended from college.
6. Harry raced down the street, fearing disaster.
7. My brother, a veteran of Vietnam, was the principal speaker.
8. Charles' parents, startled by his appearance, called their son a radical.

II. Give the plural for each of the following nouns (if necessary, consult your dictionary): *calf, potato, birch, alumna, cactus, shears, teaspoonful, Burmese, index, fish, brother-in-law, ox.*

III. Convert the possessives below, now expressed in *of* phrases, to possessives expressed by an apostrophe, or an apostrophe plus *s*. Should any of them not be changed?

1. The house of Mr. Jones and the barn of Mr. Benning were sold at the same time.
2. The leaves of many trees get summer blight.
3. The cars of my friends are new.
4. The novels of Dickens are in the reading room of the library.
5. The cost of clothes was higher at the end of the year.

[2] For a discussion of gerunds, see page 21.

6. The toys of the babies were mixed with the toys of the puppy.
7. I enjoy the poetry of Blake more than the poetry of Burns.
8. The garden of the Robinsons is carefully tended; the garden of their neighbor is not.

2. PRONOUNS: CLASSES AND CASE

A pronoun is a word that takes the place of a noun. Pronouns therefore function in sentences as nouns do—as subjects, objects, appositives, objects of prepositions, complements, and modifiers.

Pronouns may be classed as personal, relative, interrogative, demonstrative, or indefinite.

The pronouns *I, you, he, she, we, they,* and *it* with all their forms (*me, mine, we, ours, us,* etc.) are called **personal pronouns.** They are inflected for gender, number, case, and person. When the word *self* or *selves* is added to a form of the personal pronoun, the resultant form (*myself, yourself, himself, ourselves, themselves*) is called a compound personal pronoun. Such pronouns may be reflexive (I hurt *myself*) or intensive (The President *himself* will be there).

Relative pronouns are two-function words. Like other pronouns, they stand in place of a noun, but they also connect a subordinate clause to some word in the main clause. Words often used as relative pronouns are *who, whom, whose, which, what, that,* and also the compound relative pronouns *whoever, whomever, whichever, whatever.* Of these, only *who* and *whom* and their compound forms are inflected for case. Relative pronouns are sometimes understood but not expressed:

The house [*that*] he lives in is on the corner.
The man [*whom* or *that*] we expected did not come.

Who, whose, which, and *what,* when they are used to introduce a direct or indirect question, are called **interrogative pronouns:**

Who wants another piece of pie? [Direct question]
They wondered *who* had taken the money. [Indirect]

This and *that* and their plurals *these* and *those* are called **demonstrative pronouns** when they are used to point out or call attention to a particular thing:

This is the last stop.
Those are not my shoes.

Certain pronouns which do not refer to definite persons or things are called **indefinite pronouns.** Examples are: *any, nothing, few, each, much, all, something, everyone.*

> *Each* should work for the good of *all.*
> *Everyone* is to bring *something.*

The case of a pronoun is determined by its function in its clause.

a. A personal pronoun is in the subjective case when it serves as a subject of a verb or as a complement of the verb *to be* **(i.e., a predicate nominative), or when it is in apposition with a subject or with a complement of** *to be.*

> *Subject of a verb: I* wonder where *he* has gone.
> *Complement of* to be: I believe that it was *she.*
> *In apposition with a subject:* Two applicants—Richard and *I*—were interviewed by the committee.
> *In apposition with a complement:* Only one person is the criminal, *he,* Marvin.

Although the complement of the verb *to be* is in the subjective case in formal usage, the colloquial *it's me* in place of the formal *it is I* is standard English.

b. A personal pronoun is in the objective case when it is the object of a verb, a verbal,[3] or a preposition; when it is in apposition with an object; or when it is the subject of an infinitive.

> *Object of a verb:* The students admire *him.*
> *Object of a verbal:* Finally remembering *me,* Harold smiled and shook hands.
> *Object of a preposition:* They laughed at *her.*
> *In apposition with an object:* The family met us—Hilda and *me*—at the airport.
> *Subject of an infinitive:* I didn't expect *him* to come.

c. A personal pronoun is in the possessive case when it expresses possession or when it is used to modify a gerund.

> Jane is wearing *her* skirt and *my* sweater.
> Everyone regretted *his* receiving the prize. [In this sentence the gerund *receiving* is the object of *regretted,* and *his* modifies *receiving.*]

d. The case of a relative or interrogative pronoun is determined by its function in its own clause.

> Give the ball to *whoever wants it.* [*Whoever* is the subject of the italicized subordinate clause in which it appears and so is properly in the subjective case. The subordinate clause is the object of the preposition *to.*]
> If we have a party, *whom shall we ask?* [*Whom* is in the objective case because it is the object of the verb *ask.* Many students of usage, though, would defend the use of *who.*]

---

[3] If necessary, see "Verbs and Verbals" page 20.

The sentences below further illustrate some of the common problems involving case of pronouns.

He says that *we* freshmen must work together. [*We*, the subject of *work*, is in the subjective case.]

To *us* freshmen the sophomore rules seem unreasonable. [*Us* is the object of the preposition *to*.]

We were surprised to see James and *him* together after their quarrel. [Both *him* and *James* are objects of the infinitive *to see*. The use of the subjective *he* in such an expression should be avoided.]

He is a man *who*, I believe, will have his own way. [*I believe* is a parenthetical expression. *Who* is the subject of the subordinate clause *who will have his own way.*]

I saw *him* waving to his children. [*Him* is the object of *saw; waving* is a participle modifying *him*.]

We objected to *his* walking on our new lawn. [The gerund *walking* is the object of *objected to; his* modifies *walking*.]

They wondered *whom* he was taking to the dance. [*Whom* is the object of *taking* and is appropriate in formal English. In informal English and particularly in conversation, *who* can be defended.]

It wasn't Harold that asked the question; it was *I*. [*I* is here a complement of *was*, and strict formal usage therefore requires *I* rather than *me*. Some cultivated people would use *I*, some would use *me*, and many others would simply avoid the construction.]

He is taller than *I*. [Here *I* is in the subjective case because it is the subject of the elliptical clause *than I am tall*.]

EXERCISES

Underscore the preferable pronoun in each sentence. Explain your choice.

1. Will you join my parents and (I, me) for dinner?
2. The teacher would not start the lecture until (we, us) students quieted down.
3. The program was planned to help (we, us) students.
4. It is not necessary to ask (who, whom) will be the leading actor.
5. He wanted Martha and (I, me) to come.
6. Choose (whoever, whomever) you think can handle the job.
7. Such ruffians as (they, them) cause trouble for the rest of us.
8. If I were (they, them) I should refuse to buy an inferior stone.
9. Will you let Tom and (I, me) take the car?
10. (Him, his) arriving so late caused a good deal of comment.
11. He pointed out the man (who, whom) he said had helped him.
12. For some time there has been a coldness between Marion and (I, me).
13. We found (him, his) working on his term paper.
14. We found (him, his) watching television every night an annoyance.
15. I am grateful to (whoever, whomever) has worked on the program.

3. PRONOUNS: AGREEMENT   Agr

Some pronouns—indefinite pronouns, for example—do not customarily have and do not require antecedents; words like *anyone* and *everyone* are not dependent for meaning on a noun that has preceded them. Most pronouns, however, are used as substitutes for nouns and are dependent on those nouns, their antecedents, for their meaning. The antecedent is the word or words that would have to be repeated if the pronoun were not used.

A pronoun agrees with its antecedent in gender, number, and person.

Some problems of pronoun agreement stem from differences between formal and colloquial usage. Since words like *everyone, anyone, nobody* are grammatically singular, in formal usage they are followed by singular verbs and referred to by singular pronouns. Such words are, however, often plural in meaning, and in colloquial usage they are often followed by plural pronouns:

> *Formal:* Everyone did *his* duty.
> *Colloquial:* Everyone did *their* duty.

The principles of agreement stated below are based on the formal usage which most instructors will want their students to observe in written English.

a. In formal English, expressions that require a singular verb (*each, every, either, neither, many a, a person, anyone, everyone, no one, someone, anybody, everybody, nobody, somebody*) require a singular pronoun when they serve as antecedents.

> *Each* of us has *his* private anxieties and *his* private joys.
> Almost *everybody* in college knows that *he* will need to earn *his* living some day.
> If *either* Martin or Ted hears of this, *he* will oppose it.
> *Everyone* took off *his* hat and stood in silence while the body of the great man was lowered into the grave.

b. The masculine pronoun (*he, his, him*) is generally used to refer to a singular antecedent which is both masculine and feminine in meaning.

> In this small coeducational college *a student* soon learns to speak to everyone *he* meets. [Although some of the students are girls, *he* (rather than *he or she*) is the preferable usage. *He or she* would be used only for a special emphasis.]

c. Collective nouns as antecedents may be followed by *it* or *they*. If the collective noun is thought of as a unit, *it* (or the possessive form, *its*) is the appropriate pronoun; if the collective noun is thought of as representing a group of individuals, *they* (*their, them*) is the appropriate pronoun.

> The jury will give *its* verdict today. [The jury is thought of as a unit.]
> The jury are returning to *their* homes today. [A group of individuals.]

d. When *one* is the antecedent, it usually is followed by *he* or *his*.

One should weigh *his* words when *he* speaks to the council.

In very formal style, a *one* . . . *one* sequence may be used:

One regrets that *one* is unable to do more.

e. The relative pronoun *who* is generally used to refer to people and not to things; *which* is generally used to refer to things and not to people; and *that* is used to refer to people or to things or to both.

> a man *who* or *that* . . .
> a house *which* or *that* . . .
> the same man and the same house *that* we saw yesterday . . .
> a group *which* or *that* meets every Saturday . . .
> a group of home owners *who* object to their taxes . . .
> the cat *that* ate the goldfish . . .

Since there is no possessive form for *which* or *that*, the possessive of *who* (*whose*) is often used to refer to things; "the dog *whose* master has abandoned him" is preferable to the awkward *which* construction: "the dog the master *of which* has abandoned him."

f. Inconsistencies in pronoun usage should be avoided. Inconsistencies are unnecessary and undesirable shifts from one person to another, from one number to another, or from one gender to another. Some inconsistencies can be corrected by substituting the right pronoun; others call for more substantial revision.

> INCONSISTENT IN PERSON: When *I* was a freshman, the sophomores were strict in making *them* follow the rules. *You* were not safe if *you* walked on the grass or wore a high-school letter or failed to say "Sir" to upperclassmen. [A shift from the first person *I*, to the third person *them*, to the second person *you*. For consistency and for clarity this passage should be written in the first person.]
> CONSISTENT: When *I* was a freshman, the sophomores were strict in making *us* follow the rules. *We* were not safe if *we* walked on the grass or wore a high-school letter or failed to say "Sir" to upperclassmen.
> INCONSISTENT IN PERSON: When *a man* is hungry, *you* aren't satisfied with a frilly salad and a cup of tea. [A shift from the impersonal *a man* to the indefinite second person *you*.]
> CONSISTENT: When *a man* is hungry, *he* is not satisfied with a frilly salad and a cup of tea.
> INCONSISTENT IN NUMBER: *Everyone* in the class was looking at *his* watch. *They* thought the end of the hour would never come. [A shift from the singular *his* to the plural *they*. This passage could be improved by substituting *he* for *they*, but it still would not be entirely satisfactory.]
> REVISED: *Everyone* in the class was looking at *his* watch and thinking that the end

of the hour would never come. [*Or*] *Everyone* in the class was looking at *his* watch. It seemed that the end of the hour would never come.

INCONSISTENT IN GENDER: The dog barked and showed that *it* wanted to come in. I think that *he* remembered me. [A careless shift from *it* to *he*.]

CONSISTENT: The dog barked and showed that *he* wanted to come in. I think that *he* remembered me.

EXERCISES

Point out any errors or awkwardness in agreement between pronoun and antecedent in the following sentences, and correct the sentence by supplying the proper pronoun or, if necessary, by revising the sentence.

1. Each man and woman in the audience thought that the speaker had given them something to think seriously about.
2. Many a high-school boy will wish that they had studied more in high school and had prepared themselves better.
3. Everyone in the congregation gave as much as they could when the collection was taken.
4. The senior class was proud of its part in introducing the honor system.
5. The person chosen, whether a man or a woman, will find that the group will cooperate with them and will appreciate their service.
6. We saw the prisoners which had been leaders in organizing the penitentiary's baseball team.
7. No one was eager to give their time to the new organization.
8. One should practice the speech thoroughly so that they will be less nervous about facing the audience.
9. The committee made its report and said that their judgment was unanimous.
10. If any student considers the rule unfair, he or she should speak to a member of student council; they are always willing to listen.

4. PRONOUNS: REFERENCE   Ref

A pronoun should refer clearly to its antecedent. Writing becomes inexact and confusing when a pronoun may refer to more than one antecedent, when it is too far from its antecedent for clarity, or when it seems, because of its position, to refer to the wrong antecedent. Inexact thinking as well as inexact expression is often responsible for obscure or ambiguous reference. The most common types of faulty reference are:

a. Reference to an antecedent that is implied but not stated.

UNSATISFACTORY: Leslie has been interested in medicine since he was ten years old, and he plans to be *one* someday. [The pronoun *one* has no expressed antecedent.]

REVISED: Leslie has been interested in medicine since he was ten years old, and he plans to be a doctor someday.

b. Reference to a too-remote antecedent. If the pronoun and its antecedent are so distant from one another that the relationship is not immediately clear, the sentence or the passage should be revised by changing the construction or by substituting a noun for the vague or ambiguously used pronoun.

UNSATISFACTORY: She wore a ribbon on her hair *that* was green and crisp and new. [*That* appears to refer to *hair*.]
REVISED: On her hair she wore a ribbon *that* was green and crisp and new.

UNSATISFACTORY: The Supreme Court decided that the judge had shown prejudice in the case. Justice Holmes retired soon after. *That* made legal history, and lawyers argued over the case for years afterwards. [The reference of the pronoun *that* is obscure, but the sense of the sentence suggests that the pronoun is intended to refer to the court decision though the antecedent *decision* is not expressed. The passage should be revised.]

c. Ambiguous reference. The reference of a pronoun is ambiguous if the reader wavers even momentarily in choosing between two or more possible antecedents.

AMBIGUOUS: She refused to return the ring, *which* was what he wanted. [Does *which* refer to the ring or to her refusal to return it?]
REVISED: He wanted the ring, but she refused to return it. [*Or*] He was glad that she refused to return the ring.

AMBIGUOUS: The manager told the union official that it was not *his* duty to collect the union dues. [In this sentence it is not clear whether *his* refers to *manager* or to *union official*. Unless the context of such a sentence makes clear the reference of the pronoun, the sentence should be recast.]
REVISED: The manager told the union official that the union should collect its own dues. [*Or*] The manager said to the union official, "It is not my duty to collect dues for the union."

ACCEPTABLE: Mr. Thompson told his son that *he* could not join a fraternity unless *he* got better grades. [Here the reference of *he* and *he* causes no uncertainty; the general sense of the sentence makes the meaning immediately clear.]

d. Indefinite reference of *you*. In formal English the use of the pronoun *you* in the sense of *one* is out of place. In informal English the indefinite *you* can sometimes be used to give a sense of immediacy; misused, however, it may be incongruous and even ludicrous.

INAPPROPRIATE: Chaucer, born in the fourteenth century, wrote for his own age and for succeeding ages. He understood the psychological tensions of the Pardoner, though he lacked the organized psychological knowledge which is available to twentieth-century writers. *You* are astonished as *you* . . . [The indefinite and too-informal *you* is out of place in formal, impersonal writing of this kind.

More appropriate than *You are astonished as you* . . . would be *The reader* or *The modern reader* or *One* followed by *is astonished as he reads* . . .]

INAPPROPRIATE: Human nature is funny. Even if *you* have held up a bank and killed seven men, *you* may still be very gentle with your dog. [Here the *you* is undesirable because it involves the reader in a situation in which he has no part and in which, probably, he would prefer not to be involved. The writer does not really intend to address the reader; he has simply used *you* vaguely in order to get out of a difficulty.]

REVISED: Human nature is unpredictable. Even a man who has held up a bank and has killed seven men might still be very gentle with his dog.

EFFECTIVE: If *you* could have been present in the years of Barnum's greatest glory, *you* would have seen Annie Oakley . . . ; *you* would have watched Buffalo Bill . . . ; *you* would have heard the whoops of fleeing Indians and pursuing cowboys . . . ; *you* . . . etc. [Here the use of *you* serves to give the reader a more vivid sense of being present; use of the formal *one* would be out of place in this context.]

e. Reference to an inconspicuous or buried antecedent.

AWKWARD: The apartment house is the largest building on the street; it is the narrowest street in town. [*Street*, the antecedent of *it*, is buried in a prepositional phrase, and the reader expects *it* to refer to *apartment house*, the subject of the first clause.]

REVISED: The apartment house is the largest building on the narrowest street in town.

EXERCISES

Some of the following sentences are satisfactory. Others illustrate the faulty reference or the indefinite use of pronouns. Correct all unsatisfactory pronoun references. If necessary, recast the sentence.

1. In our school they don't let you smoke.
2. My mother said that my sister was an impudent child, and that she would see to it that she would never let her temper get out of control again.
3. While we were watching the man fishing on a pier, we saw him haul one in.
4. John is studying law because his father is one.
5. Whoever is going had better sign his name.
6. Mr. Banker bought John a coat but he thought it was too small for him.
7. Mary told her sister that she was not responsible for her actions.
8. The lightning struck the tree nearest the barn, but after burning for a few seconds it was extinguished by the rain.
9. The penalties for stealing are severe, but you don't usually think about penalties until after you are caught.
10. Jack gave him five dollars when he was a freshman in college.

11. The furniture van had not arrived, the telephone was still disconnected, and there was no food in the house. The dog was sick, too. This was very depressing.
12. Never beat a dog with your hand; use a newspaper; this will make him afraid of you.
13. She was angry when he tried to give her advice, which was not very helpful.
14. If you think Dick needs money, you should do it in a diplomatic way.
15. He carried the kitten in his car that was only three weeks old.

5. VERBS: PRINCIPAL PARTS Prin

Verbs are words that assert, or express action, state of being, or occurrence; they are inflected to indicate tense, voice, mood, person, and number.

a. The principal parts of a verb supply the basic forms for all tenses of that verb.

The principal parts are three: (1) the present infinitive, *climb,* (2) the past tense, *climbed,* and (3) the past participle, *climbed.* On the basis of the way they form the past tense and past participle, verbs are classified as regular or irregular. A regular verb, like *climb,* forms the past tense and past participle by adding *d, ed,* or *t* to the present infinitive. An irregular verb is one that forms its past tense or past participle in some other way; for example, *go* (present infinitive), *went* (past tense), and *gone* (past participle). Regular verbs are more common than irregular verbs, but some of the most commonly used verbs are irregular.

b. To use the information given by the principal parts of verbs, it is necessary to know at least the following facts:

(1) The first principal part (*go*) supplies the form for the present tense (first and second person, singular, *go;* third person singular, *goes;* first, second, third person plural, *go*) and the present participle, *going,* and forms the future tense (*shall* or *will go*) with the help of the auxiliary *shall* or *will.*

(2) The second principal part (*went*) supplies the form for the past tense (*went*).

(3) The third principal part (*gone*) combines with auxiliaries to form the present perfect tense (*has* or *have gone*), the past perfect tense (*had gone*), and the future perfect tense (*shall* or *will have gone*).

Many errors in tense are caused by ignorance of principal parts or by failure to choose the proper principal part. One who writes *He drownded* for *He drowned* simply does not know the principal parts of *drown.* In *He come* for *He came,* the error is produced by the use of the first principal part instead of the second; in *He had went* for *He had gone,* the error is produced by the use of the second principal part instead of the third to form the past perfect tense.

c. In revising their papers, students should look up in the dictionary the principal parts of any verb about which they are uncertain.

Dictionaries may differ in their way of indicating principal parts, but any satisfactory dictionary supplies the information and explains in an introductory section headed "Explanatory Notes" or "Inflected Forms" what system is used.

d. Students should be sure that they know the principal parts of the verbs most commonly used:

PRESENT INFINITIVE	PAST TENSE	PAST PARTICIPLE
awake	awoke	awaked
	awaked	awoke
		awakened
begin	began	begun
bid (to offer)	bid	bid
bid (to command)	bade	bidden
	bid	bid
break	broke	broken
bring	brought	brought
burn	burnt	burnt
	burned	burned
burst	burst	burst
choose	chose	chosen
come	came	come
dive	dived	dived
	dove (*colloquial*)	
do	did	done
dream	dreamt	dreamt
	dreamed	dreamed
drink	drank	drunk
drive	drove	driven
drown	drowned	drowned
dwell	dwelt	dwelt
	dwelled	dwelled
eat	ate	eaten
fall	fell	fallen
fly	flew	flown
forget	forgot	forgotten
		forgot
freeze	froze	frozen
get	got	got
		gotten

VERBS: PRINCIPAL PARTS

PRESENT INFINITIVE	PAST TENSE	PAST PARTICIPLE
give	gave	given
go	went	gone
hang (a thing)	hung	hung
hang (a person)	hanged	hanged
	hung	hung
kneel	knelt	knelt
	kneeled	kneeled
lay (to place)	laid	laid
lead	led	led
lie (to recline)	lay	lain
lie (to make a false statement)	lied	lied
light	lighted	lighted
	lit	lit
lose	lost	lost
pay	paid	paid
raise (to lift)	raised	raised
rise (to get up, to come up)	rose	risen
see	saw	seen
set (to place)	set	set
shine	shone	shone
	shined	
show	showed	shown
		showed
shrink	shrank	shrunk
	shrunk	shrunken
sing	sang	sung
	sung (*rare*)	
sit	sat	sat
slay	slew	slain
slink	slunk	slunk
spit	spit	spit
	spat	spat
steal	stole	stolen
strive	strove	striven
	strived	strived
swim	swam	swum
tread	trod	trod
		trodden

PRESENT INFINITIVE	PAST TENSE	PAST PARTICIPLE
wake	woke	waked
	waked (*rare*)	woke
		woken (primarily British)
wear	wore	worn
weave	wove	woven
wring	wrung	wrung
write	wrote	written

EXERCISES

Underscore one of the words in parentheses and give the reason for your choice.

1. The boat (lay, laid) on its side in the harbor.
2. The boys had (swam, swum) about thirty yards before they reached the shore.
3. After you (sit, set) the book on the table, (lie, lay) down on the couch and take a nap.
4. When the seams (burst, bursted), she knew she had (wore, worn) the coat long enough.
5. The man (bid, bidded) five dollars for the chair.
6. As soon as the sun (rose, raised), we took the flag and (rose, raised) it on the flag pole.
7. After I had (laid, lain) in bed for two hours, I (waked, woken) and (lay, laid) out the clothes I wanted to wear for dinner.
8. When we have (given, give) our share, we still will not have (payed, paid) our full debt.
9. The sun (shone, shoned) and the birds (drank, drunk) from the fountain.
10. For many years he had (wore, worn) the coat which had been (weaved, wove, woven) in his native land, and he (wrung, wrang) his hands in grief when it was (stole, stolen) from him.

6. VERBS AND COMPLEMENTS

A predicate is a word or group of words which makes an assertion about a subject. In sentences like *Time flies* and *Who cares?* the verbs alone constitute a predicate. Other verbs require the help of noun or adjective structures to complete the thought and establish the meaning of the verb. The helping noun or adjective is called the complement of the verb.

A *transitive* verb takes an object (He *felled* the *tree*); transitive verbs therefore take complements, since a direct object may be called a complement. *Intransitive* verbs, except for a special kind called *linking* verbs, do not take complements. Words frequently used as linking verbs are *be, seem, become, appear,* and the verbs of the senses (*smell, feel, taste, look, sound*). They are called linking because they join or link their subject to a noun or adjective. The same verb may, in different sentences, be a transitive verb, a simple (i.e., non-linking) intransitive verb, or a linking verb. Note the use of the verb *sound* in these sentences:

Used as a transitive verb: Sound the trumpets. [Sound is followed by its direct object and complement, *trumpets.*]
Used as a simple intransitive verb: The alarm *sounded.* [Here *sounded* needs no complement.]
Used as a linking verb: Your suggestion *sounds* good. [Here *sounds,* an incomplete predicate, links *suggestion* to the adjective *good. Good* is a complement.]

a. Complements of transitive verbs. Since complements of transitive verbs ordinarily present no problems of grammar or usage, we shall simply list the most common complements. They are: (1) the direct object (Eleanor was sharpening a *pencil*), (2) the indirect object (He gave *me* a ticket), (3) the objective complement (The board made him *chairman.* Jack Sprat and his wife licked the platter *clean*), and (4) the subjective complement after a passive verb (He was made *chairman* by the board. He was made *uneasy* by the decision).

b. Complements of linking verbs: the subjective complement. The complement of a linking verb, called the subjective complement, may be a pronoun, a noun or noun-equivalent (word, phrase, or clause), or an adjective (word, phrase, or clause).

It is *Tom.* [*Tom* is a predicate noun and the subjective complement of *is.*]

His objection is *that travel costs are too high.* [A noun clause used as a predicate noun, the subjective complement of *is*]

Lobbing is *returning a ball in a high curve.* [A gerund phrase used as a predicate noun, subjective complement of *is*]

She is *tall* and *graceful.* [Subjective complements of *is,* these two predicate adjectives modify the subject, *she.*]

The materials are *of the best quality.* [An adjectival phrase, used as the subjective complement of *are*]

Two difficulties may arise in connection with linking verbs. The first is that when the subjective complement is a pronoun, it is, in formal usage, in the subjective case to agree with the subject of the sentence: *This is he, that is she.* In colloquial usage, the pronoun-complement is often given the objective case, particularly in the expression *It's me.*

The second difficulty stems from the fact that a number of verbs may be used both as simple intransitives and as linking verbs; as simple intransitives they may be modified by adverbs, and as linking verbs they may have adjectives as complements. The following sentences will illustrate:

The dog smells good. [He has a pleasing odor. *Smells* is a linking verb, *good* an adjective-complement.]

The dog smells well. [He has a good sense of smell. *Smells* is an intransitive verb, *well* an adverb.]

She looked intent. [She appeared to be concentrating. *Intent* is an adjective following a linking verb.]

She looked intently. [She used her eyes to look fixedly at something. *Intently* is an adverb modifying *looked*.]

For further discussion of adjectives and adverbs, see page 33.

EXERCISES

Distinguish between adverbs and adjective-complements in the following sentences. Assuming that the sentence is grammatically correct, what does it mean, or what might it mean in a larger context?

1. The bell sounded loud.
2. The bell sounded loudly.
3. John came slowly.
4. John is slow.
5. Janet looked happy.
6. Janet looked happily.
7. Ralph appeared cautiously.
8. Ralph appeared cautious.
9. She looked careful.
10. She looked carefully.
11. The child is well.
12. The child is good.

7. VERBS AND VERBALS

Verbals may be generally defined as word forms that combine some of the characteristics of verbs with the characteristics of another part of speech. Verbals differ from verbs in that (1) verbs can undergo change in person and number, and verbals cannot; (2) verbs can make an independent predication or assertion, and verbals cannot.

a. Participles. Participles are usually defined as verbal adjectives. They have some of the characteristics of verbs: they can be transitive or intransitive, complete or linking, active or passive, and they can take complements and be modified by adverbs. In their work as adjectives, they modify nouns and pronouns and in general perform adjective functions. Forms of the participle are *knowing* and *having known* (active), and *being known, known,* and *having been known* (passive).

Three difficulties may arise in connection with participles:

(1) The confusion of participles used as verbals and participles that are part of a verb phrase. Used with auxiliaries in verb phrases, participles can be verbs and can make an independent predication; used as participles they cannot:

> Elsie has been *eating* between meals. [*Has been eating* is a verb phrase; it serves as the simple predicate of the sentence.]
>
> Joe hurried into town, *eating* a sandwich as he walked. [*Eating* is a participle modifying *Joe;* it does not serve as a predicate.]

Failure to distinguish between participles and verb phrases can produce fragmentary sentences.

(2) Dangling or misplaced participles. Participles should refer clearly to the noun or pronoun they modify.

> DANGLING: Running across the campus, the bell rang.
> REVISED: Running across the campus, I heard the bell.
>
> MISPLACED: Leaping and growling, I saw the dog as I approached.
> REVISED: I saw the dog leaping and growling as I approached.

(See "Modifiers," page 48.)

(3) Awkward participial structures used in place of a clause:

> AWKWARD: Al being an old friend, I knew I could trust him.
> REVISED: Since Al was an old friend, I knew I could trust him.

b. Gerunds. The gerund may be defined as a verbal noun. The forms of the gerund are identical with the forms of the participle, but it is usually easy to distinguish between the two if one remembers that the participle has the functions of an adjective and the gerund has the functions of a noun.

> **Gerund:** *Remembering* names is difficult for Gerald.
> **Participle:** Finally *remembering* the man's name, Gerald crossed the street and spoke to him.
>
> [In the first sentence *remembering* is the subject of *is,* and is modified by the adjective *difficult; names* is the direct object of the gerund. In the second sentence the participle *remembering* modifies the noun *Gerald* and is itself modified by the adverb *finally.*]

In their capacity as nouns, gerunds serve as subjects, objects, and complements of verbs, and in general perform the functions of a normal noun. Gerunds resemble verbs in that they can be transitive or intransitive, complete or linking, active or passive, and can have adverbial modifiers and complements in the same way that verbs can.

In formal usage, nouns and pronouns modifying gerunds are generally in the possessive case.

> *John's leaving* was a shock to her; *his coming back* is what she lives for.
> We resented *Don's consulting* the faculty committee.

In colloquial usage this convention is often ignored, and the objective rather than the possessive case is used. The objective case is appropriate in any kind of usage when stress is placed on the noun or pronoun:

> Can you imagine *Jim deciding* to go to graduate school? [The sense is "Jim of all people," or "Jim who has never seemed interested in study."]

Also, usage is divided when the modifier of the gerund is inanimate:

> The *barn's burning down* was a great loss to Mr. Johnson.
> [*Or*] The *barn burning down* was a great loss to Mr. Johnson.

c. Infinitives. The infinitive may be defined as a verbal that functions as a noun (*To live* is *to come* nearer to death), an adjective (There is a man *to admire*), or an adverb (He went *to ask* for information). It is commonly, though not always, preceded by *to*. As a verbal, the infinitive can be transitive or intransitive, complete or linking, active or passive; it can take complements and be modified by adverbs; it can also take a noun or pronoun as a subject and form what is loosely called an infinitive clause (We asked *him to bring the oars*). Like other verbals, it cannot form a complete predication. The forms of the infinitive are: *to forgive* and *to have forgiven* (active), and *to be forgiven* and *to have been forgiven* (passive).

When an infinitive is used as a modifier, it should, like a participle, refer clearly to the noun or pronoun it modifies.

> FAULTY: To flower in June, you should set out the plants by the middle of May.
> REVISED: To flower in June, the plants should be set out by the middle of May.

The *split infinitive* occurs when a modifier is placed between *to* and the other part of the infinitive: "to industriously work." Split infinitives should be avoided whenever they can be avoided without loss of effectiveness or accuracy; usually the modifier can with advantage be placed either before or after the infinitive.

> AWKWARD: It was strange to, without really trying, succeed.
> REVISED: It was strange to succeed without really trying.

> AWKWARD: He tried to cautiously determine how much she had heard.
> REVISED: He tried cautiously to determine how much she had heard.

The split infinitive is not, however, the sin against good usage which it has sometimes been labeled. Sometimes splitting an infinitive is necessary to preserve exact meaning. An authority on usage, George O. Curme, gives this example of an infinitive that must be split for the sake of exactness: "He failed to entirely comprehend it." Neither "He failed entirely to comprehend it" nor "He failed to comprehend it entirely" would have the same meaning.

EXERCISES

I. Identify the verbs, participles, gerunds, and infinitives in the following sentences.

1. Undisturbed by the clamor around him, Elmer continued to eat his supper.
2. Jean's arriving so early gave her hosts a problem to solve.
3. To waver is to risk losing what we have tried to win.
4. Having been thwarted in his efforts to see Linda, Bob, still determined, decided to write a letter to her.
5. Reading the assignment twice is a good procedure to follow.
6. Reading the assignment a second time, Bert had the feeling of mastering the material.
7. We asked her to bring the sandwiches, knowing that being asked would give her pleasure.
8. Having learned that Helen hated walking, I did not dare suggest walking to town.
9. Practicing makes the work easy to do.
10. We protested her leaving the party, and finally persuaded her to stay and go home with us later.

II. Revise the sentences below to eliminate the faulty or awkward use of participles, gerunds, and infinitives.

1. Walking along the road, the sun came up over my right shoulder.
2. To study efficiently, the room should be cooler.
3. Falling over the goal line, the touchdown was made.
4. He intended to quickly and quietly leave.
5. The days are long when doing unpleasant work.
6. To be productive, you should plant tomatoes before the first of June.
7. Him refusing to go aroused her anger.
8. Mary being my guest, I consulted her about the plans.
9. Jack said that laughing was good for the soul. Laughing as he said it.
10. He tried to superstitiously avoid walking under the ladder.

8. VERBS: AGREEMENT   Agr

A verb agrees with its subject in person and number.

Sentences in which the subject immediately precedes the verb and in which the subject is clearly singular or clearly plural offer no problems of agreement. Mistakes in agreement most often occur when intervening words blur the subject-verb relationship, when the verb precedes the subject, or when the writer is not sure whether a particular subject should be considered singular or plural.

Conventions that govern the agreement of the verb with its subject differ in formal and informal usage. In applying the rules listed below, the student should be aware that a number of them are flexible, and that a sentence in which a rule is mechanically followed may be stiff or awkward and may need to be recast.

a. A verb agrees with its subject in person and number—not with an expression mistakenly considered to be its subject.

(1) A verb agrees with its subject—not with a modifier of the subject.

The destruction of the ships and landing forces *has* [not *have*] *been accomplished.* [The subject is *destruction.*]

My understanding of many ideas *has* been clarified. [The subject is *understanding.*]

(2) A verb agrees with its subject—the number of the verb is not influenced by the subjective complement.

The problems of municipal government *are* [not *is*] his chief interest. [The plural subject, *problems*, requires a plural verb. If the subjective complement, *interest*, were made the subject, the sentence would read: "His chief *interest is* the problems of municipal government."]

(3) A verb agrees with its subject—the number of the verb is not influenced by phrases introduced by *with, in addition to, along with,* and the like.

The *man* with his six children *is* [not *are*] waiting at the door.
The *teacher* as well as the students *finds* the room too warm

In sentences like these, there seems to be an awkward disagreement between formal grammar and meaning. For this reason many people prefer to recast the sentences to make the subject plural:

The man and his six children *are* waiting at the door.
The teacher and the students *find* the room too warm.

(4) A verb agrees with its subject—not with the introductory adverbs *here* and *there.*

Here *come* the *professor and* his *wife.* [*Come* is plural because it agrees with the compound subject.]
Here *comes Dean Harlow.*
There *sits* our most distinguished *citizen.*
There *lie* our *enemies.*

(5) A verb agrees with its subject—not with the expletive *there*.

There *is* only one *reason* for their quarrels.
There *are* several *reasons* for his decision.

Two qualifications of this convention should be noted. In spoken English the convention is often waived, and one hears sentences like "There's Tom and Betsy." In written English, usage is divided when a sentence has an expletive and a verb followed by a series, the first item of which is singular: "In the room there *were* (or *was*) a scarred desk, a straight chair, and a couch with sagging springs."

b. Singular subjects joined by *or* or *nor* take a singular verb.

He did not know whether the *captain* or the *lieutenant was* responsible.
Neither *Arthur* nor his *father was* at home.

c. When a singular and a plural subject are joined by *or* or *nor*, the verb agrees with the nearer subject.

He did not know whether the *officer* or the *soldiers were* to blame.
He did not know whether the *soldiers* or the *officer was* to blame. [Sometimes following this convention will produce "correct" but awkward sentences. Such sentences should be recast to avoid the construction.]

d. When two subjects joined by *or* or *nor* differ in person, the verb agrees with the nearer subject.

Either James or *I am* willing to go.
Neither John nor *you are* capable of dishonesty.

Such sentences, too, are frequently awkward, and it may be wise to recast them:

Both *James and I are* willing to go.
John is not capable of dishonesty, nor *are you*.

e. Singular subjects joined by *and* take a plural verb unless the subjects are thought of as a unit.

Honesty and justice are required in a judge.
My *guide and counselor* [one person] *has served* me well.

f. The pronoun *each* and compound subjects modified by *each* and *every* take a singular verb.

Each of the carpenters *is bringing* his own tools.
Each magazine and newspaper has its special place on the stand.
Every tree and every bush was coated with ice; *every street was* dangerously slippery.

g. Collective nouns may take either singular or plural verbs, depending

upon whether they are thought of as referring to a single unit or to the individuals in the group.

> The *committee is meeting* this morning. [The committee is thought of as a unit.]
> The *committee are arriving* tonight and tomorrow, some by train and some by plane.
>
> The *number* of errors *accounts* for the grade.
> A *number* of students *are* leaving early.
>
> A *majority is* needed before a vote can be taken.
> The *majority were* on their feet before the vote was called for.

h. The pronouns *none* and *any* may take either singular or plural verbs, depending upon the sense of the sentence.

> None of the grass *was* burned.
> None of the leaves *are* raked.
>
> Any of these dates *is* convenient.
> Any of us *are* invited.

i. In mathematical calculations either a singular or a plural verb may be used.

> Two plus two *is* (or *are*) four.
> Three and three *is* (or *are*) six.

j. The antecedent of the relative pronouns *who*, *which*, and *that* determines the number and person of the verb of which the pronoun is the subject.

> It is *I who am* to blame, and it is *you who deserve* the praise.
> She is one of those determined *women who insist* on having the last word.[4]

k. In formal usage *one*, *no one*, *anyone*, *everyone*, and *someone*, and *nobody*, *anybody*, *everybody*, and *somebody* require singular verbs.

> *No one was* willing to bring up any new business because *everyone was* eager for the meeting to come to an end.
> *Everyone*—even the older people who did not dance—*was* having a good time at the party.

EXERCISES

In the following sentences, point out any subject-verb agreement that should be corrected in formal written English and revise any sentences that need revision.

---

[4] Margaret M. Bryant notes that although about five out of every six writers use the plural (one of those who *are*) in sentences of this kind, the singular (one of those who *is*) is also used by educated writers and occurs frequently in informal English. *Current American Usage*, p. 12.

1. Each voter in these three communities are planning to cast a ballot in this election.
2. My cousin along with several friends from New York are going to pay us a visit.
3. There is, the senator says frequently and forcibly, many reasons why all good citizens should vote.
4. Neither the president nor his representatives were able to attend the ceremony.
5. Neither of the professors were able to answer my question.
6. Every doctor and every dentist in town are free on Wednesday afternoons.
7. Each of the fighters were becoming tired by the end of the fifth round.
8. Everyone—male and female, young and old—like to attend barn dances.
9. He is one of those men who is called successful but who is merely rich.
10. War may be eliminated when the causes of war is understood.
11. Either Harry or I are ready to volunteer.
12. Neither he nor his partner are entirely blameless.
13. This collection of essays have been carefully chosen.
14. There's Janice and her brother.
15. Her principal interest are books.

9. VERBS: VOICE AND MOOD

Voice

Voice is the property of the verb which shows whether the subject of the verb acts or is acted upon. Active voice shows the subject acting; passive voice shows the subject acted upon.

Active voice: Our team *won* the game.
Passive voice: The game *was won* by our team.

The passive voice is useful, particularly when the doer of the action is unknown or is relatively insignificant. For example, the sentence "Someone has stolen the *Mona Lisa* again" is less effective than the passive statement "The *Mona Lisa* has been stolen again." Often, though, the passive is unemphatic, indirect, wordy, and vague. Since active statements are frequently more effective, one should use the passive only when there is good reason for doing so.

Weak passive: Current events were discussed and long papers were written by us.
Active: We discussed current events and wrote long papers.

Weak passive (and unnecessary shift to passive in the middle of the sentence): As we entered the woods, a shot was heard.
Active: As we entered the woods, we heard a shot.

Mood

Mood is the property of the verb which indicates whether the speaker is (1) making a request or giving a command (imperative), (2) expressing a supposition or wish (subjunctive), or (3) stating a fact or opinion or asking a question (indicative).

> **Imperative mood:** *Close* the window. Then please *sit* down.
> **Subjunctive mood:** If I *were* wealthy I could own a yacht.
> **Indicative mood:** His son *is* at home now. *Will* he *stay* long?

Some problems with mood arise in connection with the subjunctive, a mood little used in modern English. In some situations, however, it may be necessary to make a choice between the indicative and the subjunctive. Conventions for the use of the subjunctive are:

a. The subjunctive is used to express a condition that is contrary to fact.

> If I were you, I should accept the invitation.
> Even if he were wealthy, he would still wear old clothes.
> He would pay his share if he were able.

b. The subjunctive may be used to express strong doubt.

> *Subjunctive:* If it should be a rainy day, we shall not go. [Since the speaker is expressing doubt that the day will be rainy he uses the subjunctive.]
> *Indicative:* If it is a rainy day, we shall not go. [The indicative is used because the idea of doubt is not emphasized.]
>
> *Subjunctive:* If the teacher were to give a quiz, some of us would be sorry. [This sentence implies that the speaker does not expect the quiz to be given.]
> *Indicative:* If the teacher gives a quiz, some of us will be sorry. [This sentence does not indicate whether or not a quiz is likely.]

c. The subjunctive is used in *that* clauses expressing a recommendation, a demand, a request, a necessity.

> The committee recommended that the project be abandoned.
> He demanded that the bill be paid immediately.
> He asked that we be quiet.
> They demand that the rules be changed.
> I move that the petition be granted.
> It is essential that this law be passed.

Sentences like those just above can often be recast to avoid the formal subjunctive:

> The committee recommended abandoning the project.
> He demanded immediate payment of the bill.
> He asked us to be quiet.
> They demand a change in the rules.
> Passage of this law is essential.

The subjunctive also survives in modern English in certain exclamations and wishes like "so *be* it," "far *be* it from me to object," "peace *be* with you," "Heaven *help* us all."

VERBS: TENSE   29

Unnecessary shifts in mood—from indicative to imperative or imperative to indicative, for example—can produce awkward sentences.

EXERCISES

I. Change the following passive statements to active statements. How many of them are improved by use of the active voice?
1. Your invitation was received by me today.
2. On the athletic field, students playing hockey can be seen.
3. By nine o'clock the book was read, the cat was put out, and he had gone to bed.
4. When the bell rang, students pouring out of the buildings were observed.
5. The President was elected by a large majority.

II. In each of the following sentences, choose the verb that seems preferable, and justify your choice.
1. The law requires that the defendant (have, has) benefit of counsel.
2. If the earth (was, were) square, some nations would want all four corners.
3. I wonder if the young man who just spoke to me (was, were) a college student.
4. Senator Borgam Patwell moved that the motion (be, was) postponed indefinitely.
5. Rosalind would like Russell better if he (were, was) a better correspondent.
6. If Thornton (was, were) ever kind, he was kind for a reason.
7. I should go for a swim today if the water (was, were) not so cold.
8. What could I say if the professor (was, were) to ask why I have been absent?
9. He requires that each student (give, gives) a five-minute speech.
10. The man asked if it (were, was) too late to get a ticket for the game.

10. VERBS: TENSE

The six main tenses of English verbs are:

Present tense: I walk.
Past tense: I walked.
Future tense: I shall (will) walk.
Present perfect tense: I have walked.
Past perfect tense: I had walked.
Future perfect tense: I shall (will) have walked.

The simple present tense often indicates habitual or timeless action: *I walk to school every day. Snow falls early in Maine.* The form *I am walking,* which indicates action occurring at present, is called the progressive present; and a third form of the present, *I do walk,* is called the emphatic present. The past tense has corresponding forms: *I was walking. I did walk.* Past action is also sometimes recorded in the present tense, or historical present. Future time is frequently expressed by constructions other than the future tense; for example: *I am going to walk, I expect to walk soon, I am about to walk.*

Knowledge of the following conventions will help to prevent the misuse of tenses.

a. Statements regarded as permanently true are expressed in the present tense.

>In the first grade the child learned that two and two *are* [not *were*] four.
>Socrates believed that the unexamined life *is* not worth living.
>
>People in the ninth century thought that the world *was* flat. [The past tense is correct here because the speaker does not regard the idea as true now.]
>
>Copernicus discovered that the earth *revolves* [not *revolved*] around the sun.

b. The historical present tense may be used effectively in the presentation of lively dramatic action, but is likely to be inappropriate when used for routine narrative.

> APPROPRIATE: A crowd has assembled now and is peering up at the man on the ledge of a tenth-story window. Other tenth-story windows are open, filled with gesticulating and shouting people. The man on the ledge is shaking his head. Now he has turned and is looking at the street below him. Suddenly . . .
>
> PROBABLY NOT APPROPRIATE: Before me on the library path I see Henry. I hardly recognize him under that battered old hat, and apparently he doesn't even see me. I pass him and go on to my history class.

c. Generally the past tense is used to refer to action completed in the past, and the past perfect is used to refer to action completed prior to some definite time in the past.

> When I *called* he *had* already *left.* [*Called,* past tense, represents action completed in the past. *Had left,* past perfect, represents action completed prior to the past action described by the verb *called.*]

d. The present perfect tense represents an action occurring at an indefinite time in the past and extending up to and perhaps through the present time.

> Richard *has been* on the honor roll three times. [*Has been* here means up to the present time.]
>
> Helen *has been waiting* for him to call. [This sentence implies that she is still waiting.]

e. The future perfect tense represents an action to be completed in the future prior to a definite time in the future.

> I *shall have left* before you arrive.
> By next week, all the students *will have gone* home.

f. The tense of subordinate clauses should be in logical sequence with the tense of the main verb.

I *had been* in college for two months before I *met* him. [Since being in college preceded the meeting, the past perfect tense and the past tense are properly used to show the time-relationship of events.]

I *think* that you *will* do well.

I *thought* that you *would* do well.

g. The time indicated by infinitives and participles should be adjusted to the tense of the main verb and the meaning of the sentence.

I was glad *to receive* the letters. [I.e., I was glad *when I received* the letters.]

I was glad *to have received* the letters. [I.e., at some time in the past I was glad that I *had already received* the letters.]

Having waited in the rain for three hours, Mark *was* thoroughly exasperated when Helen finally appeared. [Not "Waiting in the rain for three hours, Mark was thoroughly exasperated when Helen finally appeared." Since waiting preceded and caused the exasperation, the action referred to by the participle is previous to that of the verb, and the form *having waited* is therefore required.]

Casting fearful glances behind him, the boy *walked* by the graveyard. [Here the action of the participle and the action of the main verb occur simultaneously and the present participle is properly used.]

h. When direct discourse is changed to indirect discourse, the tense of verbs should be adjusted.

Direct discourse: Sara said, "I *love* to study history."
Indirect discourse: Sara said that she *loved* to study history.

Direct discourse: He asked, "*Have* you a date for Saturday night?"
Indirect discourse: He asked if I *had* a date for Saturday night.

Direct discourse: Dave said, "I *had planned* to go home this weekend until I *heard* from my parents."
Indirect discourse: Dave said that he *had planned* to go home this weekend until he *heard* from his parents. [Here the verbs are unchanged; there is no way of giving *had planned* a greater degree of past time, and *heard* must remain in the past tense to preserve the logical sequence of tenses.]

Shall and *Will, Should* and *Would.* Usage is divided on *shall* and *will* and on *should* and *would.* In formal usage, many careful writers still attempt to preserve some of the distinctions between them, and feel strongly that the distinctions should be made; other careful writers use *will* in place of the more formal *shall,* and *would* in place of the more formal *should.* In informal English, *will* and *would* are more commonly used; and it is often possible to use contractions (*I'll, I'd, he'll,* etc.) and so to avoid the problem. Statements **a** and **b** below describe traditional, formal usage.

a. To express simple futurity, *shall* (or *should*) is used in the first person and *will* (or *would*) in the second and third persons.

I shall (should) go.	We shall (should) go.
You will (would) go.	You will (would) go.
He, she, it will (would) go.	They will (would) go.

b. To express determination, promise, or command, *will* is used in the first person, and *shall* is used in the second and third persons.

I will.	We will.
You shall.	You shall.
He, she, it shall.	They shall.

c. *Would* may be used in all persons to express determination.

He warned me, but I *would* have my way.
I warned him, but he *would* have his way.
He warned you, but you *would* have your way.

d. *Should* may be used in all persons to express possibility or supposition.

Even if I (you, he) *should* be defeated, the cause will not be lost.

e. *Should* in the sense of *ought to* is used in all three persons.

If we are to consider our duty, you *should* go, I *should* go, and he *should* go.

f. *Would* is used in all persons to express habitual action.

I (you, he) *would* stop each day to see the progress the workmen had made on the new office building.

EXERCISES

I. Point out misuses of tense in the sentences below and revise any sentences that need revision.

1. These primitive people did not know that the world was round or that three and three made six.
2. Did you call him yet?
3. Marrying the editor's daughter, he was surprised when he learned that he was to start to work as office boy in the editorial department.
4. Pausing in the middle of his speech, he glanced at Ted and beckoned to him.
5. Although Carlyle wrote many volumes, he often said that silence was greater than speech.
6. At the dance that night there were many of the people that we saw in the afternoon.
7. The sky was gray and the wind shook the trees. The sun, which was shining this morning, is now obscured.
8. I called her each night ever since we went to the game together.
9. They have completed the project several days ago. Now they have started work on the new tunnel.

10. Although he was really terrified the night before, he now tried to pretend that he felt very calm.
11. Crossing the room, he opened the door.
12. Before the first of the month, he finishes his term paper.
13. Mary had been in college a year before she had learned how to study.
14. Walking past the housemother's room, Ida answered the telephone.
15. I have done so well in my courses last term that I decided to take an extra course this term.

II. Consider the use of *shall* and *will,* and *should* and *would* in the following sentences. Some of the uses are clearly correct; some are clearly incorrect; some are matters of taste; some could be correct if the sentence were interpreted in a certain way. Classify each sentence and comment on it. Correct any uses that are clearly wrong.

1. He shall attend the dinner if it is held at a convenient place and time.
2. Will you go to the party?
3. They are very likely to come, but what if they would be late?
4. I will be pleased to accept your invitation.
5. I will drown unless someone shall save me.
6. They should have come earlier; now the dinner is cold.
7. I warned him, but he would not listen.
8. When we were children, we would meet Father at the gate and he would give us sticks of candy.
9. He gave us the key in case he should not be there to let us in.
10. I should like to attend the concert but I don't think I will be able to go.
11. I would always help him when he would have let me.
12. We should have known that they should try to mislead us.

11. ADJECTIVES AND ADVERBS Adj, Adv

Adjectives (words, phrases, and clauses) modify nouns and pronouns. *Descriptive* adjectives express a quality, condition, or characteristic of the noun or pronoun:

> The man, *old* and *stooped,* is still *vigorous.* [*Old* and *stooped,* apposed adjectives, and *vigorous,* a predicate adjective, characterize *man.*]

Limiting adjectives point out or identify particular members of a class:

> *This* man and *three* boys delivered *the* furniture to *my* house. [The four italicized words function as limiting adjectives.]

Adverbs (words, phrases, and clauses) usually modify a verb, an adjective, or another adverb. Sometimes they modify a whole sentence rather than a particular expression in the sentence:

> *Possibly* she has forgotten what day it is.

Simple adverbs supply answers to such questions as How? When? How much? Where? In what order or degree?

> She slept *late.*
> He talked *slowly.*
> Our work is *somewhat* harder *here* than it was *there.*
> He came *first* and stayed *longer* than anyone else.

Interrogative adverbs (*when, why, how, where*) introduce a question:

> *Where* did he go? *Why* has he gone?

A *conjunctive* adverb (sometimes called a transitional adverb or sentence connector) acts as a conjunction and at the same time acts as an adverb in that it modifies the action of its clause. Expressions commonly used as conjunctive adverbs are: *besides, indeed, in fact, also, moreover, furthermore, nevertheless, still, however, therefore, thus, hence, consequently, accordingly.*

> His nose was broken; *nevertheless* he fought on.
> They were very late; *in fact* they arrived when the dance was over.

Adjectives and adverbs are inflected to show degree of comparison:

> **Positive degree:** *young* brother, *courageous* man, runs *fast,* moved *quickly.*
> **Comparative degree:** *younger* brother, *more courageous* man, runs *faster,* moves *more quickly.*
> **Superlative degree:** *youngest* brother, *most courageous* man, runs *fastest,* moves *most quickly.*

Some words are compared irregularly, by a change in form: *good, better, best; little, less* (or *lesser*), *least.*

Understanding of the following principles will help to avoid the misuse of adjectives and adverbs.

a. Adverbs modify verbs which express action. Adjectives serve as subjective complements of linking verbs (i.e., verbs that express little or no action and serve primarily to link the subject to what follows). Words often used as linking verbs are *be, seem, become, appear,* and the verbs of the senses (*smell, taste, feel, look, sound*).

> He *carefully* avoided the broken glass. [In this sentence it is clear that *carefully* is an adverb modifying *avoided.* This sentence presents no problem.]
> He looked *steadily* at the papers before him. [*Looked* is sometimes used as a linking verb, but here it is used to describe or convey action, and the adverb *steadily* tells how he *looked*—i.e., how he performed the action.]
> She looks *happy.* [Here *looks* serves only to join the subject *she* to the adjective *happy* and is a linking verb: it describes the subject and not the action. *Happy* is a subjective complement.]
> That small boy looks *mischievous.* [*Mischievous,* a subjective complement, describes the boy.]
> The small boy looked *mischievously* at his companion. [*Mischievously* describes the act of looking.]

He is doing *well* [not *good*] in his history course. [*Good* would be wrong here because an adverb is needed to modify the verb *is doing*.]

I can't tell whether he feels good or *bad*. [*Badly* in place of the adjective *bad* is often used colloquially.]

He felt his way *uncertainly* in the darkened room. [*Felt* describes an act; *uncertainly* describes how that act was done.]

b. With transitive verbs, adjectives may serve as objective complements—i.e., may serve to modify the object in a particular way.

She cooked the meat *tender*. [*Tender*, an adjective, applies to the state of the meat and is correct. To substitute *tenderly* for *tender* would be to change the sense of the sentence.]

She cooked the meat *quickly*. [*Quickly* is not an objective complement but is an adverb modifying *cooked*.]

We painted the barn *red*. [*Red*, an adjective, applies to the state of the barn and is an objective complement.]

c. Dictionaries supply important information about particular adverbs and adjectives.

One cause of errors in the use of adverbs and adjectives is uncertainty as to which part of speech a particular word may be. Can *slow*, for example, be used as an adverb? Looking up the word in a good dictionary will reveal that it is used as an adjective or as an adverb. If one looks up the word *considerable* he will learn that it is an adjective (or, colloquially, a noun) and not an adverb. Dictionaries also supply information about the way adverbs and adjectives form the positive, comparative, and superlative degrees.

d. Adjectives and adverbs should not be overused.

Adjectives and adverbs (and expressions used as adjectives or adverbs) are of course indispensable, but they should be used economically and exactly. When they are overused, they tend to clutter communication and to obscure the essential ideas. The skillful writer usually depends upon effective verbs and nouns to carry most of his meaning. He uses adjectives and adverbs to qualify and to make more precise the work done by verbs and nouns.

Overuse of modifiers is most likely to occur in pretentious or generally wordy expression. The best way to avoid this fault is to write honestly and unaffectedly, and to strike out or to express more briefly words, phrases, or passages that do not carry their share of meaning.

EXERCISES

I. In each of the following sentences choose one of the words in parentheses and explain the reason for your choice. (Sometimes the choice may depend on the sense intended.)

1. Mary plays golf as (well, good) as John does.
2. When you get to know her, she is a (real, really) sincere person.
3. Morris does not feel (good, well) about it; and Melvin, I understand, feels (bad, badly) and is very unhappy.
4. After weighing each of the three sisters, we discovered that Helen was the (heavier, heaviest).
5. Did the ride on the merry-go-round make you feel (bad, badly)?
6. He held the boat (steady, steadily).
7. That fish smelled (peculiar, peculiarly) to me.
8. You look (considerable, considerably) better today.
9. Although the dog looks gentle, he hears strangers however (quietly, quiet) they move, and he barks (ferocious, ferociously).
10. She looked (sick, sickly) to me.
11. He thought that he had been treated (bad, badly).
12. I have trouble with chemistry but I am doing very (good, well) in English.
13. She may smile (pleasant, pleasantly) now, but she looked (miserable, miserably) this morning.
14. He is the (older, oldest) of the three Harris boys.
15. He walked (slowly, slow) and (cautiously, cautious) down the dark road.

II. Write the comparative and superlative degrees of the following adjectives and adverbs.

far	tired	safe
beautiful	much	slow
gladly	handsome	slowly
old	bad	pleasant

12. CONNECTIVES Con, Conj

Prepositions

A preposition is an expression used to connect a noun or pronoun to some other element in the sentence. The noun or pronoun, called the object of the preposition, may be a word, a phrase, or a dependent clause. A preposition may be a single word (*on, in, along,* etc.) or several words (*in accordance with, because of,* etc.).

He argued *with* me. [*With,* a preposition, takes as its object the pronoun *me* to form the prepositional phrase *with me.*]

a. Prepositions should be used idiomatically.

Certain words are conventionally joined to certain prepositions to form idiomatic phrases. For example, *accuse* is followed by *of* (*accuse* him *of* the crime); *acquiesce* is followed by *in* (*acquiesce in* a decision); and *wait* is followed by *on* or *for* (*wait on* a customer, *wait for* a friend or a bus). Dictionaries give information about idiomatic usage, and the student should look up a word when he is uncertain about the preposition that conventionally follows it.

b. A preposition may be used at the end of a sentence. The effort to avoid prepositions at the ends of sentences sometimes produces awkward constructions. *We had many things to talk about* is a more natural sentence than *We had many things about which to talk.* If natural rhythm and idiom place a preposition at the end of a sentence, no convention of good usage requires that the sentence be changed.

Conjunctions

A conjunction is an expression that connects words, phrases, or clauses. Conjunctions differ from prepositional connectives in that prepositions always have an object expressed or understood and conjunctions do not.

>He was tired, *for* it was very late. [*For* is a conjunction joining two independent clauses. It does not have an object.]
>He did the work *for* five dollars. [*For* is a preposition, and its object is *dollars.*]

Conjunctions may be classified as *coordinating conjunctions, subordinating conjunctions,* and *conjunctive adverbs.*

Coordinating conjunctions connect elements of equal rank. The most common connectives of this kind, sometimes called pure conjunctions, are *and, but, for, or, nor. So* and *yet* may also be used as pure conjunctions.

>He is young *and* strong. [*And* connects *young* and *strong.*]
>The two nations fought on the land *and* on the sea. [*And* connects two phrases.]
>He may be old, *but* he is still a good swimmer. [*But* connects two independent clauses. In a sentence of this kind, a comma conventionally precedes the coordinating connective; if the comma is not needed for clarity or emphasis, it may be omitted.]
>Chester was late, very late. *And* Ann resented it, although she said nothing at the time. [*And* connects two sentences.]

Certain coordinating conjunctions are used in pairs and are called correlative conjunctions. Examples are *not only . . . but also, either . . . or, neither . . . nor, both . . . and.*

>*Both* Ted *and* I are going.
>*Neither* he *nor* she wants to marry.

Subordinating conjunctions connect clauses of unequal rank and show the relationship between them. Subordinating conjunctions are *after, although, as, because, before, if, since, so that, that, though, unless, until, when, where, whether, while.*

He did not speak *because* he was angry. [*Because* subordinates *he was angry* and connects it with the main clause of the sentence.]

When the situation is clearer, I can make a decision. [*When* connects the subordinate clause of which it is a part to the main clause *I can make a decision*.]

Conjunctive adverbs (also called transitional adverbs, transitional connectives, and sentence connectors) join two independent clauses or sentences, and at the same time modify the clause or sentence in which they occur. Expressions used as conjunctive adverbs are *accordingly, again, all the same, at the same time, also, besides, consequently, conversely, furthermore, for that reason, hence, however, indeed, in fact, likewise, moreover, nevertheless, notwithstanding, on the other hand, on the contrary, on that account, otherwise, rather, still, then, therefore, thus.*

The student council has refused to act; *for that reason* we are circulating a petition.

He is unmoved by emotional appeals; he is ready, *however*, to listen to reason.

The lectures stimulated discussion both on the campus and in town; the students are eager, *therefore*, to continue them next year.

The sentences above illustrate two points worth noting about conjunctive adverbs. (1) When a conjunctive adverb is the sole connective between two independent clauses in the same sentence, it is generally preceded by a semicolon. (2) Conjunctive adverbs, unlike coordinating and subordinating conjunctions, are movable; they do not necessarily stand at the head of the clause to which they belong, and a sentence is frequently improved when a conjunctive adverb is moved out of the emphatic head position.

a. Conjunctions should express clearly and exactly the relationship the writer intends.

The overuse or imprecise use of conjunctions like *as, so, while, and, but,* and *since* often produces ineffective writing. *As*, for example, is often used where *because,* or *for,* or *when,* or *since,* or *just as* would more clearly express the meaning. *So* is often used in sentences where *so that,* or *accordingly,* or *for this reason* would be more precise. *While* is sometimes used inexactly for *but* or *although*. *And* carries the general meaning of addition or continuity, but expressions like *consequently* and *again* may serve better in particular contexts. *But* is not always the best expression of contrast; sometimes *yet,* or *nevertheless,* or *however,* or *on the contrary* may be preferable. *Since* may be less exact than *because* or *for* in some sentences. The following sentences illustrate imprecise uses of conjunctions:

As I was on the beach, I could see the approach of the storm. [This sentence is ambiguous. It may mean *When* I was on the beach . . . or *Because* I was on the beach . . .]

While the road was very dark, we knew it well and could find our way. [*While*

is essentially a time-connective; *although* would be more exact in this sentence.]
She received the letter *and* she called her parents. [*And* is a loose connective here. *When* she received . . . or, *As soon as* she received . . . would more clearly establish the relationship of the two clauses.]

b. Conjunctions should be appropriate to the style of a piece of writing.

In the following sentences, heavy and incongruous connectives are used inappropriately in simple, informal writing:

POOR: *Notwithstanding the fact that* he weighs only one hundred and fifteen pounds, Larry is a good athlete.
IMPROVED: Although he weighs only one hundred and fifteen pounds, Larry is a good athlete.

POOR: We didn't know *whence* the hired man came, or how long he would work for us.
IMPROVED: We didn't know where the hired man came from, or how long he would work for us.

POOR: I wasn't sick after eating the green apples, *whereas* Helen and Tom missed two days of school.
IMPROVED: Although I wasn't sick after eating the green apples, Helen and Tom missed two days of school.

POOR: My room, *albeit* small and dark, is the only place in the house where I can work in peace.
IMPROVED: My room, though small and dark, is the only place in the house where I can work in peace.

On the other hand, certain connectives widely used in colloquial English are not appropriate in written English unless the style is intended to sound colloquial. Among those connectives is *like* used as a conjunction in place of *as* or *as if* ("Write the paper *like* I told you to write it."). Comments on *like* and other dubious connectives can be found in the Glossary of Usage, pages 124–140.

EXERCISES

I. Choose the idiomatic prepositions in the following sentences. If necessary, consult your dictionary.

1. We knew that he was capable (of, for) doing the work well.
2. The child was accompanied (with, by) his mother.
3. He is willing to abide (by, with) the rule.
4. Jack dissented (with, from) the majority.
5. My hat is identical (with, to) yours.

6. Bob is oblivious (of, to) the irony of the situation.
7. Sam is proficient (at, in) mathematics.
8. His misplaced humor is repugnant (for, to) me.
9. We all concur (in, with) the decision.
10. Dave is angry (with, at) all his friends.

II. Comment on the exactness and appropriateness of the connectives in the following sentences, and revise any sentences that need revision.

1. As I was driving to school, I decided to stop and see Mary.
2. Harold's brothers played golf and tennis while he enjoyed reading.
3. We're going hiking on Saturday; moreover we hope to do some mountain climbing Sunday.
4. I knew that he was guilty as I saw him fire the shot.
5. He looks like his father, but he talks like his mother does.
6. Dorothy has been depressed since Alec went to New York without saying goodbye.
7. We began to worry about her as it was near midnight.
8. I saw in the paper where another plane crashed.
9. I felt that she was deceitful as I heard her evade Ralph's questions.
10. He hurried so he would not be late.
11. She is an attractive girl, if she is not a good student.
12. My roommate makes the beds while I clean up the room.
13. Mrs. Boone is always sociable and pleasant; conversely, Mr. Boone is not.
14. He was on probation last term, and he is spending more time on his studies now.
15. Being as the weather was warm, we planned to have the party outdoors.

13. PHRASES AND CLAUSES

a. A phrase is a group of two or more grammatically related words which does not contain a subject and a predicate and which functions as a single part of speech.

> *Noun phrase:* *Talking to her friends* is one of her chief pleasures. [The italicized phrase is the subject of the verb *is.*]
> *Verb phrase:* By one o'clock he *will have finished* his examination. [The phrase consists of *finished,* the main verb, and its auxiliaries, *will* and *have.*]
> *Adjectival phrase:* She lives in the house *with green shutters.* [The phrase modifies the noun *house.*] *Smiling sourly,* she watched him go. [The phrase modifies the pronoun *she.*]
> *Adverbial phrase:* He executed the order *without delay.* [*Without delay* tells how he executed the order and so modifies the verb *executed.*]

b. A dependent (or subordinate) clause is a group of words which has a subject and a predicate, but which is a dependent part of a sentence.

PHRASES AND CLAUSES

Like phrases, dependent clauses do the work of a single part of speech, and they may be called noun or adjective or adverb clauses.

> *Noun clause:* He denied *that life is short.* [The clause serves as the object of *denied.*] I know *he will come.* [*He will come* looks like an independent clause, but it is easy to see that the word *that*—I know *that* he will come—is understood here though it has been omitted. *That he will come* is the object of the verb *know,* and the clause is therefore a noun clause.]
> *Adjective clause:* I returned to the town *where I was born.* [Modifies the noun *town.*]
> *Adverbial clause:* The students celebrate *when examinations are over.* [Modifies the verb *celebrate.*]

c. An independent (or main) clause has a subject and predicate and makes, with the help of context, a complete assertion.

A simple sentence consists of one independent clause; a compound sentence of two or more independent clauses; a complex sentence of one independent clause and one or more dependent clauses; a compound-complex sentence of two or more independent clauses and one or more dependent clauses. An independent clause, therefore, may be a complete simple sentence, or part of a compound, complex, or compound-complex sentence. It may also be an absolute construction—a construction grammatically unrelated to the rest of the sentence.

> *Dogs chase cats.* [This is a simple sentence as well as an independent clause.]
> *Jonathan's father loves his son,* but *he loves his car too.* [Two independent clauses form a compound sentence.]
> Tom said—*everyone listened intently*—that the film was banned in Boston. [The italicized clause is an absolute construction in a complex sentence.]

EXERCISES

Identify independent and dependent clauses in the following sentences.

1. Where you go I will go.
2. He said the weather was sure to improve.
3. Ruth cut the flowers, and Jane arranged them.
4. This is what he wants, and he is determined to have it.
5. I said, though it wasn't true, that I would miss him.
6. What you ask is almost impossible for us to do when we think what the consequences might be.
7. He robbed the bank while his confederates stood guard outside and the police were eating lunch.
8. The examination I took was very difficult.

9. Because the moonlight was beautiful and the night was warm, we stayed on the lake until everyone else had gone.

10. You may leave whenever you wish, but be sure you get home early.

14. FRAGMENTARY AND INCOMPLETE SENTENCES   PF, Frag

According to the broadest definition, a sentence is any locution spoken or punctuated as an independent unit of discourse. For practical purposes, we can say that a sentence is grammatically complete when it contains a subject and a predicate and, in context, makes an independent assertion.[5]

a. A fragmentary sentence is an unsatisfactory incomplete sentence. It is a subordinate part of a sentence written with a capital letter at the beginning and a period at the end.

The error of punctuating a fragmentary sentence as if it were a complete sentence is called the **Period Fault.** Basically, though, fragmentary sentences are produced, not by poor punctuation, but by the failure to recognize the elements of a sentence; most fragments result from the confusion of verbs and verbals, or the confusion of phrases or dependent clauses with independent clauses. Sometimes a fragment needs simply to be attached to the preceding or following sentence, of which it may be a dependent part; sometimes it needs to be rewritten so that it becomes an independent statement.

> UNSATISFACTORY: He arrived late. *Having been detained at the office.* [A participial phrase written as a sentence]
> REVISED: Having been detained at the office, he arrived late.
>
> UNSATISFACTORY: I enjoy realistic writers. *Like Saul Bellow and John O'Hara.* [A prepositional phrase written as a sentence]
> REVISED: I enjoy realistic writers like Saul Bellow and John O'Hara.
>
> UNSATISFACTORY: I am taking three sciences. *Biology and chemistry and geology.* [Appositives written as a sentence]
> REVISED: I am taking three sciences: [or a dash] biology, chemistry, and geology.
>
> UNSATISFACTORY: At three o'clock he was ready to leave. *When suddenly he saw her hurrying through the crowd.* [A dependent clause written as a sentence]
> REVISED: At three o'clock he was ready to leave. Suddenly he saw her hurrying through the crowd.

Fragmentary sentences like those above force the reader, who has learned to expect the completion of an idea within the conventional signs of the sentence, to stop and mentally correct the writing. Such fragments are considered

---

[5] Statements in the imperative mood *(Shut the door. Be ready at six.)* are classified as complete sentences even though the subject, *you*, is not expressed.

errors because they indicate incompetence; they suggest that the writer does not know the difference between a sentence and a part of a sentence.

b. Some grammatically incomplete sentences convey clearly and appropriately the meaning the communicator wishes to convey.

Such sentences are more common in informal than in formal writing. Exclamations, questions, answers to questions, certain transitional expressions, established formulas, and bits of dialogue are often quite properly written as sentences:

What an examination!

Questions? Of course I had questions. What I needed was answers, and I sought those answers in my reading.

Is our policy the correct one? *Perhaps so.* We need, though, to be aware of certain obstacles.

To return now to the causes of this act of aggression. [A transitional phrase leading into a new paragraph]

Nothing ventured, nothing gained. [A familiar formula]

Going to the play tonight?
No. Have to study. Exam tomorrow.

Also, in narrative writing, particularly in modern fiction, one may find an impressionistic setting down, in incomplete sentences, of a character's thoughts, or of descriptive detail:

It was a beautiful calm day. *Not a ripple on the water. Not a cloud in the sky.*

Deciding what can properly be punctuated as a sentence involves, like many other matters of English usage, the application of good judgment rather than rigid rules about what is and what is not an acceptable sentence. Since the careless or illiterate fragmentary sentence is jarring to an educated reader, many English instructors require students to mark with an asterisk any incomplete sentences they use, and to indicate in a note at the bottom of the page that the incomplete construction is intentional. Students whose sense of style is unsure will be wise to avoid incomplete sentences except in exclamations and in the writing of dialogue.

EXERCISES

I. In the passages below (1) revise or repunctuate any fragmentary sentences, and (2) point out any acceptable incomplete sentences and explain why you think they are acceptable.

1. Mr. Wilder is a self-made man. Having worked hard all his life and accomplished a great deal.
2. Let me help you. Since I happen to be here.
3. Knowing that she should apologize for her rudeness but lacking courage to face him after what she had said.
4. Chester is not planning to attend the dance. Because of financial difficulties.
5. Being deeply indebted to his godfather, Horace decided to give him a present. A wrist watch. Which would have permanent value. Hoping very much that his godfather would be pleased.
6. Rain on the windows. Rain sluicing down the street. The world was dismal with rain.
7. To my surprise, I received a C. Thus doing better than Albert.
8. Whether it was good or bad he didn't know. But at least it was over now. Settled, once and for all.
9. Would the Dean believe that the car had really broken down? Probably not.
10. Although eager to go, uncertain about what awaited me when I got there.
11. He came at nine. When I had given up hope.
12. Dorothea made a poor impression. In every way.
13. I missed the test. As a result of being ten minutes late to class.
14. Some columnists should be jailed for libel. Charles B. Muddle, for example.
15. I hope to be elected to Phi Beta Kappa. Chiefly to please my parents.
16. He was happily married, he enjoyed his work, he had high hopes for the future. Then the sudden disaster.
17. Though reading the material several times, still not comprehending it as well as I should.
18. Van studies till twelve-thirty every night. Being the studious type.
19. Jim spent all his money in Miami. Easy come, easy go.
20. The heat shimmered up from the pavement. Shimmered from the low buildings and the parked cars.

II. Read the passage below, with particular attention to the incomplete sentences. Why do you think the author chose to use them? What would be the effect on the passage of adding verbs to make the sentences grammatically complete?

Fog everywhere. Fog up the river, where it flows among green aits and meadows; fog down the river, where it rolls defiled among the tiers of shipping, and the waterside pollutions of a great (and dirty) city. Fog on the Essex marshes, fog on the Kentish heights. Fog creeping into the cabooses of collier-brigs, fog lying out on the yards, and hovering in the rigging of great ships; fog drooping on the gunwales of barges and small boats. Fog in the eyes and throats of ancient Greenwich pensioners, wheezing by the firesides of their wards; fog in the stem and bowl of the afternoon pipe of the wrathful skipper, down in his close cabin; fog cruelly pinching the toes and fingers of his shivering little 'prentice boy on deck. Chance people on the bridges peeping over the parapets into a nether sky of fog, with fog all round them, as if they were up in a balloon, and hanging in the misty clouds.

Gas looming through the fog in divers places in the streets, much as the sun may, from the spongy fields, be seen to loom by husbandman and ploughboy. Most of the shops lighted two hours before their time—as the gas seems to know, for it has a haggard and unwilling look.

The raw afternoon is rawest, and the dense fog is densest, and the muddy streets are muddiest, near that leaden-headed old obstruction, appropriate ornament for the threshold of a leaden-headed old corporation: Temple Bar. And hard by Temple Bar, in Lincoln's Inn Hall, at the very heart of the fog, sits the Lord High Chancellor in his High Court of Chancery.—CHARLES DICKENS, *Bleak House*

15. FUSED AND RUN-TOGETHER SENTENCES   CF, Run

a. A fused sentence is produced when two independent clauses NOT joined by a pure conjunction[6] are incorrectly written with no punctuation between them.

> The decision is difficult to refuse to help seems selfish. [The two independent clauses—*the . . . difficult* and *to refuse . . . selfish*—are said to be fused because there is no punctuation between them.]

b. A run-together sentence (or comma fault) is produced when two independent clauses NOT joined by a pure conjunction are unconventionally written with only a comma between them.

> The decision is difficult, to refuse to help seems selfish. [Here the same two independent clauses are said to be run together because the comma is used where a heavier mark is needed.]

Fused and run-together sentences, sometimes the result of careless punctuation, are more often the result of the writer's not recognizing independent clauses or not knowing how a sequence of two independent clauses is conventionally written and punctuated. When the clauses are felt to be closely related, the relationship may be expressed in the following ways:

(1) For emphasis, the clauses may be written as independent sentences.

> They want to spend the summer in Michigan. I want to stay here.

(2) The clauses may be joined by a pure conjunction, or by a pure conjunction plus a comma.

> They want to spend the summer in Michigan, but I want to stay here.

(3) The clauses may be written without a pure conjunction and separated by a semicolon.

> They want to spend the summer in Michigan; I want to stay here.

[6] *And, but, for, or,* and *nor* are the most common pure conjunctions. *So* and *yet* may also be used as pure conjunctions.

(4) The clauses may be linked by a conjunctive adverb (*however, therefore, nevertheless, consequently,* etc.) and separated by a semicolon, or written as two sentences. A comma in place of the semicolon or period would produce a run-together sentence.

> The plan merits serious consideration; therefore it would be unwise to vote on it at this meeting.
> The prospects for the early passage of the bill are not good. Senator Wylie, however, is still hopeful.

A general rule that will help students avoid both fused and run-together sentences is: Between two independent clauses in the same sentence not joined by *and, but, for, or,* or *nor,* use a semicolon.[7]

Fused sentences are likely to produce at least momentary confusion for the reader, and they are an annoyance: the reader is forced to make the separation of ideas that the writer should have made for him. Run-together sentences, too, can be annoying and confusing, particularly when modifiers intervene between the two clauses. The following run-together sentences will illustrate:

> Their parents have consented, according to rumor, they will soon be married. [One cannot tell which of the two statements is a matter of rumor. A semicolon should be used in place of one of the commas.]
> The party started late and lasted till dawn, therefore, the guests talked about it for weeks. [Does *therefore* belong logically with the first clause or with the second? One of the commas should be a semicolon.]
> They quarreled bitterly, late that night, he called to apologize. [A semicolon should be used after *bitterly* or after *night* to indicate whether the quarrel or the apology occurred late that night.]
> He was tired, after his winter of work, he decided to take a vacation. [A semicolon is needed after *tired* or after *work* to show with which clause the phrase belongs.]

Although fused and run-together sentences can sometimes be made satisfactory simply by putting a semicolon or a period between the independent clauses, often this change in punctuation is only a superficial technical improvement. For an effective sentence, an essentially weak structure needs to be revised.

> RUN-TOGETHER: I make many mistakes in writing, most of them are in spelling and punctuation.
> TECHNICALLY IMPROVED: I make many mistakes in writing; most of them are in spelling and punctuation.

---

[7] In a series of *more* than two parallel independent clauses in a sentence, commas are generally used: *Martha is bringing sandwiches, Sue is bringing salad, and Gina is bringing cake.*

REVISED: I make many mistakes in writing, most of them in spelling and punctuation.
FUSED: Jim has a good job he has had it since July.
TECHNICALLY IMPROVED: Jim has a good job; he has had it since July.
REVISED: Jim has had a good job since July.

c. Run-together sentences may be used in special situations.

In informal English, when the clauses are short and closely related and there is no danger of misreading, sentences are sometimes run together:

Jack likes him, I don't.

In modern narrative writing, too, one not infrequently finds closely related main clauses deliberately run together to give an effect of rapid movement, breathless action, or concurrent impressions or events. The following informal passages, each written by a careful modern craftsman, will illustrate:

A few frogs lost their heads and floundered among the feet and got through and these were saved. But the majority decided to leave this pool forever, to find a new home in a new country where this kind of thing didn't happen. A wave of frantic, frustrated frogs, big ones, little ones, brown ones, green ones, men frogs and women frogs, a wave of them broke over the bank, crawled, leaped, scrambled. *They clambered up the grass, they clutched at each other, little ones rode on big ones.* And then —horror on horror—the flashlights found them.—JOHN STEINBECK, *Cannery Row*

At first the Thompsons liked it [a tune repeatedly played on a harmonica] very much, and always stopped to listen. Later there came a time when they were fairly sick of it, and began to wish to each other that he would learn a new one. *At last they did not hear it any more, it was as natural as the sound of the wind rising in the evenings,* or the cows lowing, or their own voices.—KATHERINE ANNE PORTER, "Noon Wine"

In the passage below, from an essay, the author effectively runs together independent clauses to give the impression of quick anxieties crowding the mind of the biographer:

Unfortunately for the biographer, readers will not suffer lengthy quotations. At sight of set-in paragraphs, readers flee; *they are gone, lost, the book is closed.* The thought was awful to me. *I must devise ways, I must lend a hand to my readers.* ...
—CATHERINE DRINKER BOWEN, "The Business of a Biographer"

The inexperienced writer should remember, however, that run-together sentences have no place in formal writing, that they are still widely objected to even in informal writing, and that they may be unclear. If the student wishes to use run-together sentences in informal narrative, he should probably, as with incomplete sentences, star the passage and indicate to his instructor in a footnote that his punctuation is deliberate. Students who are unsure should avoid this experimental punctuation.

EXERCISES

Correct the punctuation in the following fused and run-together sentences, and revise any sentences that would be improved by further revision.

1. Jane is a good friend when she makes a promise she always keeps it.
2. He is trustworthy, as far as I know, he has never been in trouble.
3. Today is the thirteenth of April this is my sister's birthday.
4. Mark came today to visit Steve was something he had wanted to do for a long time.
5. He is a Communist sympathizer, a man formerly associated with the Party testified to this before the committee.
6. He admired her courage above all the rest of her good qualities seemed secondary to this one.
7. I did not answer when he questioned me he eyed me suspiciously.
8. We knew what he had done, what he had intended, we did not know.
9. The boys walked slowly along the road the grass was burned.
10. This is the time of year when spring seems far away, when will winter end, we wonder.
11. He had traveled widely in this country, Latin America, and Canada, he had many friends in every part of the continent.
12. Tony has won his letter in football he is the only sophomore who has played in every game.
13. My father and grandfather were lawyers, therefore I have always been interested in law, I intend to make it my profession.
14. Ralph broke a date with Georgia last Saturday, consequently she is not speaking to him, although he has called her every night this week.
15. The international situation is not hopeless, on the contrary it seems much brighter than it did a month ago, and I have renewed faith in the United Nations.
16. He was born in 1887. He is eighty-five years old therefore he walks very slowly.
17. She told him she never wanted to see him again, moreover, she was exasperated that he even suggested a date.
18. My math teacher gave only two A's I think this is unfair.
19. John said he was resigning from the Student Council, he announced this yesterday.
20. The English book has a rule about using semicolons, in sentences like this, one can just as well use commas however, I can try it the other way.

16. MODIFIERS   DM, Mod

Modifiers should, for clarity, be close to the locution they modify, and should be so placed that they cannot appear to modify the wrong locution.

a. A modifier is called dangling when the word it logically modifies has been left out of the sentence.

(1) Dangling phrases.

DANGLING: Walking up the path, a stone lion stood in front of the museum. [According to the sentence, the lion walked up the path; the actual walker has been left out of the sentence.]
REVISED: Walking up the path, we saw a stone lion standing in front of the museum.

DANGLING: After opening the oven door, the chicken cooked more slowly. [The chicken did not open the oven door.]
REVISED: After I opened the oven door, the chicken cooked more slowly.

DANGLING: There was the village green, driving through the town.
REVISED: We saw the village green as we drove through the town.

Sentences containing dangling phrases are corrected by inserting the word that the phrase should modify (Walking up the path, *we* saw . . .), or by changing the phrase to a clause that has as its subject the real doer of the action (After *I* opened the oven door . . .).

(2) Dangling elliptical clauses. A dangling elliptical clause may be corrected by adding the words omitted in the incomplete clause.

DANGLING: When eight years old, my father was very severe about my smoking. [Since the person who was eight years old has been left out of the sentence, *When eight years old* appears to modify *my father*.]
REVISED: When I was eight years old, my father was very severe about my smoking.

DANGLING: While writing a letter to his brother, a pigeon flew into the room.
REVISED: While Jim was writing a letter to his brother, a pigeon flew into the room.

(3) Dangling infinitives.

DANGLING: To avoid eye strain, the lamp should have a hundred-watt bulb.
REVISED: To avoid eye strain, you should have a hundred-watt bulb in your lamp.

DANGLING: To enjoy television, the television room must be well planned.
REVISED: To enjoy television, one must have a well-planned television room.

b. A modifier is called misplaced when its position is such that it appears to modify the wrong word.

(1) Misplaced adverbs.

MISPLACED: He nearly wrote all of his term paper yesterday.
REVISED: He wrote nearly all of his term paper yesterday.

MISPLACED: He needed someone to help him review the material badly.
REVISED: He badly needed someone to help him review the material.

(2) Misplaced phrases.

MISPLACED: I saw a church as I walked up the hill with a white steeple.
REVISED: I saw a church with a white steeple as I walked up the hill.

MISPLACED: Snarling in anger, I saw the dog as I came into the yard.
REVISED: I saw the dog snarling in anger as I came into the yard.

(3) Misplaced clauses.

MISPLACED: I had an unhappy experience in my first year of high school which I shall never forget.
REVISED: In my first year of high school I had an unhappy experience which I shall never forget.

MISPLACED: He sat smoking his pipe on the front porch that he had just lighted.
REVISED: He sat on the front porch, smoking the pipe he had just lighted.

(4) Ambiguous modifiers.

AMBIGUOUS: When John applied for the position on the advice of his roommate he dressed very carefully. [The phrase *on the advice of his roommate* is a "squinting modifier"; its position is such that it may modify either the preceding or the following words.]
REVISED: On the advice of his roommate, John dressed very carefully when he applied for the position. [*Or*] When John, on the advice of his roommate, applied for the position, he dressed very carefully.

AMBIGUOUS: He said after the election he would take a vacation.
REVISED: After the election, he said he would take a vacation. [*Or*] He said that he would take a vacation after the election.

EXERCISES

Point out any dangling, misplaced, or ambiguous modifiers in the following sentences and revise any sentences that need revision.

1. Curled up on the sofa, the cat purred comfortably.
2. John almost shoveled all the snow from the walks and driveway.
3. When covered with syrup, you will enjoy a tasty dish.
4. She was a tall woman with black hair and a friendly smile about thirty years old.
5. After staying at home for three days, my cold was better.
6. The house was set in a pine grove with a beautiful view and blue shutters.
7. While quietly studying, the doorbell disturbed Jane.
8. After preparing for an evening alone, I heard him come in with annoyance.
9. The teacher called on Bryan to recite for the fourth time.
10. She looked at Oscar when he came in with a vacant stare, then started to play the piano again.
11. Horace found the material which the other members of the class had been unable to find in the public library.

12. After finishing high school, my father thought I should work for a year before coming to college.

13. Eleanor was criticized for taking a stand publicly against the decision of the student council by her sorority sisters.

14. I decided we should leave when the clock struck twelve.

17. FAULTY RELATIONSHIPS OF SENTENCE ELEMENTS   Cst

Most of this section is a review of faulty relationships, or constructions, discussed in other parts of the book. When a faulty relationship is treated fully elsewhere, we shall illustrate it briefly and give a reference to the fuller treatment.

a. Faulty agreement of subject and verb, or of pronoun and antecedent.

FAULTY: My *study* of history and French *have* heightened my desire to go to Paris.
REVISED: My *study* of history and *French has* heightened my desire to go to Paris.

FAULTY: The *students which* demonstrated last night are seeing the Dean today.
REVISED: The *students who* demonstrated last night are seeing the Dean today.

See "Verbs: Agreement," page 23, and "Pronouns: Agreement," page 10.

b. Faulty parallelism.

NON-PARALLEL: He objected *to the food* and *that the dining room was noisy*.
REVISED: He objected *to the food* and *to the noise* in the dining room.

See "Parallelism," page 63.

c. Misrelated modifiers.

MISRELATED: *Writing my term paper* last night, a bat flew into the room.
REVISED: *When I was writing* my term paper last night, a bat flew into the room.

MISRELATED: The man who is riding the grey *horse with a cigar* is Major Banting.
REVISED: The *man with a cigar* who is riding the grey horse is Major Banting.

See "Modifiers," page 48.

d. Poorly related clauses.

LOOSELY RELATED: Ann was determined to appear in the play, *and* she had a sore throat.
REVISED: *Although* she had a sore throat, Ann was determined to appear in the play.

AMBIGUOUSLY RELATED: *As* I was only a few miles from St. Louis, I decided to call Henry.

REVISED: *When* I was only a few miles from St. Louis, I decided to call Henry. [*Or*] *Since* I was only a few miles from St. Louis, I decided to call Henry.

See "Subordination," page 64, and "Connectives," page 36.

e. Faulty complements.

Faulty complements occur when an adverb instead of an adjective is used after a linking verb, when the noun-complement of a linking verb is not logically the equivalent of the subject, and when a pronoun-complement does not agree with the subject.

FAULTY: The garden smells *fragrantly* after the rain.
REVISED: The garden smells *fragrant* after the rain.

FAULTY: Integrity is *where one lives up to his principles.*
REVISED: Integrity is *living up to one's principles.*

FAULTY: My greatest difficulty in writing is *when I have to find a subject.*
REVISED: My greatest difficulty in writing is *finding a subject.*

FAULTY IN FORMAL USAGE: If I were *him,* I should act differently.
REVISED: If I were *he,* I should act differently.

See "Verbs and Complements," page 18.

f. Unnecessary and awkward shifts in subject, or in voice, mood, or tense of verbs.

SHIFT IN SUBJECT AND IN VOICE: When Jane went for the mail, a letter from home was found.
REVISED: When Jane went for the mail, she found a letter from home.

SHIFT IN VOICE AND IN MOOD: First sandpaper the surface carefully; then the varnish should be put on.
REVISED: First sandpaper the surface carefully; then put the varnish on.

See "Verbs: Voice and Mood," page 27, and "Verbs: Tense," page 29.

g. Inconsistency in style or usage.

SHIFT FROM PERSONAL TO IMPERSONAL STYLE: If you are diligent, you will do well; one must remember that college is primarily for study.
REVISED: If you are diligent, you will do well; you must remember that college is primarily for study.

SHIFT IN USAGE: Mrs. Grantham sought revenge by fouling up her rival's debut.
REVISED: Mrs. Grantham sought revenge by ruining her rival's debut.

h. Awkward separation of sentence elements.

Frequently, and appropriately, modifiers separate a subject and verb, a verb and its object or complement, or the parts of a verb phrase. For example, sentence elements are satisfactorily separated in the sentence: "The *secretary, it appears, is* deliberately *withholding* vital *information.*" Awkward separation of elements is needless separation that breaks the continuity and natural rhythm of the sentence.

> AWKWARD: Jane had, after a long period of unrest, uncertainty, and anxiety, decided to go.
> REVISED: After a long period of unrest, uncertainty, and anxiety, Jane had decided to go.
> AWKWARD: John went to see, when the swelling and the pain in his ankle increased, the doctor.
> REVISED: When the swelling and the pain in his ankle increased, John went to see the doctor.

i. Incomplete constructions.

Incomplete constructions occur when words that are grammatically necessary to complete the construction or the sense of the sentence are omitted.

> INCOMPLETE: I write to my closest friends *with whom* I have much in common and *know me* as I am.
> REVISED: I write to my closest friends *who know me* as I am and with whom I have much in common.
> INCOMPLETE: He both *hopes* and fears *the time of* his graduation from college.
> REVISED: He both *hopes for* and *fears the time of* his graduation from college. [*Or*] He looks forward with both hope and fear to his graduation from college.
> INCOMPLETE: Girls are more interested in clothes *than horses*. [The sentence might be understood to mean "more interested in clothes *than horses are.*"]
> REVISED: Girls are more interested in clothes *than in horses.*
> INCOMPLETE: Herbert did better on the examination than *any member* of the class. [The sentence suggests that Herbert is not a member of the class. If he is, the sentence is incomplete.]
> REVISED: Herbert did better on the examination than *any other member* of the class.

One kind of incomplete construction is used commonly, particularly in speech, and is considered standard English:

> John was *as tall* if not taller *than his brother.*

Most teachers will want their students to complete the construction in writing:

> John was *as tall as* if not taller than *his brother.* [*Or,* for a less awkward sentence] John is at least as tall as his brother.

j. Illogical constructions.

Illogical constructions occur when two things not of the same kind or construction are compared or placed in apposition.

ILLOGICAL: I like this *teacher* better than *any course* I have had.
LOGICAL: I like this teacher better than any I have had. [*Or*] I like this course better than any I have had.

ILLOGICAL: *Like most novels of Dickens, the heroine* is a generous, unsophisticated girl.
LOGICAL: This girl, like most of Dickens' heroines, is generous and unsophisticated.

ILLOGICAL: Robert's *ears are large, like his father.*
LOGICAL: Robert has large ears like his father's. [*Or*] Robert, like his father, has large ears.

ILLOGICAL: I read Carl Becker's *Modern Democracy, an historian* I greatly admire.
LOGICAL: I read *Modern Democracy* by Carl Becker, an historian I greatly admire.

k. Mixed constructions.

Mixed constructions occur when the writer carelessly fuses two different constructions.

MIXED: John's ambition is to be a lawyer and is working industriously to achieve his goal.
REVISED: John's ambition is to be a lawyer; he is working industriously to achieve his goal.

MIXED: When the chapel bell rang five times was the signal for a fire drill.
REVISED: When the chapel bell rang five times, we prepared for a fire drill. [*Or*] Five rings of the chapel bell signaled a fire drill.

EXERCISES

Revise any of the following sentences that need revision, to eliminate shifted, incomplete, and illogical constructions, and other faulty relationships of sentence elements.

1. The proposal of the students was more radical than the faculty.
2. I use my limited vocabulary as an excuse for my poor writing, though being inexcusable.
3. He was a short, bald-headed man who always looks as though he had slept in his clothes.
4. In making up an advertisement, one must be skillful, have a thorough knowledge of the product, well trained, and experienced.
5. You need more than a knowledge of the game to be a golf caddy; one must also be a student of human nature.
6. I like Audrey's perfume; she smells well.
7. If I were him, I would not change all the plans and they already made.
8. The buyer of a second-hand car should be able to recognize certain signs of

hard use; look, for example, at the floor pads and brake pedal and having in mind the condition of the springs.

9. Riding down the street, a dog ran in front of the car.
10. The grass was uncut and the blinds closed.
11. The man that is leading the dog in the leather jacket is my neighbor.
12. I am disgusted with the people he associates.
13. Joan finally, not to drag out the story too long and include every detail, decided to stay in school.
14. Robert has studied French for six years, where Martha has no knowledge of the language and not desiring to.
15. Professor Brown said in the office the papers were ready for us.
16. My reasons for writing on a topic other than the topic assigned is it did not interest me, thus making it difficult.
17. I like apples better than any fruit.
18. Tom is over at Jane's house who is his cousin.
19. After the excitement was all over was when we got there.
20. Jack thinks he will not be involved or even connected with the accident.
21. I never have and I still do not understand what a restrictive modifier is.
22. Hilary went to the headmaster for information was just what he needed to know.
23. Unlike most poetry, Robert Frost is not difficult to understand.
24. The teacher-student relationship in college is more impersonal than high school.
25. Like many other students, success in medicine is my ambition.

HANDBOOK

Section 3

STYLE AND RHETORIC: SUMMARY AND REVIEW

18. CHOICE OF WORDS
WW, Ch, Exp

The symbol **WW** (wrong word) in the margin of a theme generally means that the writer has used a nonexistent word or expression ("undoubtably"); has used a word ungrammatically ("The pipes bursted"); has fallen into inappropriate usage ("The situation was thoroughly fouled up"); has mistaken the meaning of a word ("He made no direct illusion to Russia in the speech"); or has used a word or expression loosely and inexactly ("He gave many causes for his choice"). The student should look up in the dictionary any word marked **WW**; should (if he finds it) determine its meaning and possibly its status; and should substitute in his theme a more exact or more appropriate word or expression.

Skill in the choice of words is a complex skill. The writer should:

a. Avoid padding, jargon, and vague, awkward, ill-phrased, or trite expressions.

b. Choose appropriate usage.

c. Use exact, concrete words, wherever possible, in place of abstract words (*red barn* instead of "building").

d. Use exact names (*lectern* instead of "little stand on the desk").

e. Use strong, working words (The siren *screamed* instead of "made a noise like a scream").

f. Choose words with exact connotations (She was *slender and lovely* instead of "skinny and lovely").

g. Be unsatisfied until the precise word or expression is found to convey the meaning intended.

19. COHERENCE   Coh

Coherence in writing is produced by logical order and clear connections between parts of the material.

The following passages illustrate a lack of coherence produced by faulty arrangement of material:

> POOR IN COHERENCE: We did our best to explain what had happened, to John and Carol, having arrived two hours late at the dance because we had mistaken the time.
> IMPROVED: When, having mistaken the time, we arrived two hours late at the dance, we did our best to explain to John and Carol.
> POOR IN COHERENCE: When I met him again, he appeared to have changed his mind. This was four days later, and was in the morning.
> IMPROVED: When I met him one morning four days later, he appeared to have changed his mind.

Failure to make clear connections between ideas produces incoherence in the following passages:

> POOR IN COHERENCE: Her uncle was not comforted and she left. She would go the next day.
> IMPROVED: Since she could do nothing to comfort her uncle, she left, promising to return the next day.
> POOR IN COHERENCE: He was successful for three reasons. He sold a vitamin compound and he believed it was a good product. He was sincere in this. He was

a good talker and could convince anyone on any matter and besides he liked people.

IMPROVED: He was successful for three reasons: he sincerely believed in the vitamin compound he was selling; he talked convincingly; and he liked people.

For further information related to coherence, see "Modifiers," page 48; "Faulty Relationships of Sentence Elements," page 51; "Parallelism," page 63; "Subordination," page 64; "Transitions," page 66; and "Unity and Focus," page 66.

20. CONCRETENESS   Abst

Concrete words are words referring to objects which have existence in the physical world, on the nature and meaning of which, therefore, people can to a considerable extent agree. Although abstract words (**Abst**) are necessary in discussing general concepts and conditions, concrete words are preferable, whenever they can appropriately be used, because they convey more exact factual and attitudinal meaning.

a. Concrete expression is achieved by substituting concrete words for abstract words.

ABSTRACT: The flowers were different colors.
CONCRETE: The chrysanthemums were bronze, yellow, and white.

b. Concrete expression is achieved by expanding general statements with concrete particulars and examples.

ABSTRACT: He is a good citizen.
CONCRETE: He is a good citizen. He has agreed to take charge of the Community Fund drive, and he has been chairman of the School Committee for three years.

c. Concrete expression is achieved by using concrete comparisons and figures of speech.

ABSTRACT: The length of time organic life has existed on earth is almost inconceivable.
CONCRETE COMPARISON: In order to understand the process of organic evolution, let us imagine a cord stretched from New York to Boston, each yard of which represents 10,000 years....

ABSTRACT: People cannot live isolated from other human beings.
CONCRETE FIGURE OF SPEECH: No man is an island, entire of itself; every man is a piece of the continent, a part of the main....

21. ECONOMY   Econ

a. Economy is achieved by avoiding padding and jargon.

(1) *Padding* is a term for words and phrases that add nothing but length to a sentence.

> PADDING: There are a large number of college students who find it difficult to do their work punctually on time, with the resulting effect that they receive poor marks which do not make them happy.
>
> IMPROVED: Many college students find it difficult to do their work punctually; they receive poor marks as a result.

(2) *Jargon* is a term for verbose, "heavy" language.

> JARGON: Ultimately I ascended the incline to view the conflagration.
> IMPROVED: Finally I went up the hill to see the fire.

b. Economy is achieved by cutting weak clauses to phrases or to single words.

> WORDY: Mr. Brown, who was my chemistry teacher, had a classroom manner which was very interesting.
> IMPROVED BY CUTTING CLAUSES: Mr. Brown, my chemistry teacher, had a very interesting classroom manner.

c. Economy is achieved by the substitution of exact words for longer locutions.

> WORDY AND INEXACT: She planted some bulbs of those little yellow and purple flowers that bloom early in the spring.
> CONCISE: She planted some crocus bulbs.
>
> WORDY: He looked at her with an expression of great displeasure and hostility on his face.
> CONCISE: He scowled at her.

d. Concrete detail and repetition for emphasis should not be confused with wordiness.

> BRIEF BUT UNINFORMATIVE: She seemed upset.
> IMPROVED BY ADDITIONAL DETAIL: She talked rapidly, her eyes darting from his face to the handkerchief she was twisting in her hands. In the middle of a sentence she got up and left the room.

22. EMPHASIS   Emph

a. Emphasis is achieved by proportion.

In the whole composition, main ideas are emphasized by fuller development than is accorded less significant ideas.

b. Emphasis is achieved by pause.

Pauses created by chapter divisions, paragraph breaks, and marks of punctuation throw emphasis on the material immediately preceding and following the pause.

> LESS EMPHATIC: At first I did not know what was required of me, but I know now.
> MORE EMPHATIC: At first I did not know what was required of me. I know now.

c. Emphasis is achieved by position.

The beginning and end of a composition, a paragraph, and a sentence are the positions of greatest emphasis. They should be used to stress the important ideas.

> UNEMPHATIC SENTENCE BEGINNING: There was a writer named Matthew Arnold who influenced my thinking.
> MORE EMPHATIC: Matthew Arnold was a writer who influenced my thinking.
>
> UNEMPHATIC SENTENCE ENDING: The situation is critical, I believe.
> MORE EMPHATIC: The situation is, I believe, critical.

d. Emphasis is achieved by skillful repetition.

> "This great Nation *will endure* as it has *endured, will* survive and *will* prosper. So, first of all, let me assert my firm belief that the only thing we have to *fear* is *fear* itself...."

e. Emphasis is destroyed by:

  (1) Thoughtlessly repeated sentence patterns.
  (2) Improper subordination that gives stress to ideas not worth emphasizing.
  (3) Overuse of the passive voice.
  (4) Triteness.
  (5) Padding, jargon, weak clauses, and circumlocutions.
  (6) Euphemisms overused or inappropriately used.
  (7) Abstract words thoughtlessly used.

f. Skillful writers do not rely for emphasis on mechanical devices like exclamation points, underlining, capitalization, and the use of intensives.

> POOR DEVICES FOR EMPHASIS: It happened *so suddenly!* I was a victim of Fate. *What* was I to do in these ghastly circumstances?

23. FIGURATIVE LANGUAGE   Fig

In figurative language, words are used non-literally. The basis of most figurative language is comparison or association of two ordinarily separate things or ideas.

a. The most common figures of speech are:

(1) *Simile:* a non-literal comparison, usually introduced by *like* or *as,* of two things unlike in most respects but similar in others.

> He shall come down *like rain upon the mown grass.*

(2) *Metaphor:* an implied non-literal comparison.

> I am the *captain of my soul.*
> The fog comes *on little cat feet.*
> With *rue my heart is laden* for *golden* friends I've had.
> A *dusty* answer.

(3) *Analogy:* a sustained comparison of two ideas or situations.

(4) *Metonymy:* a form of comparison in which an exact name for something is replaced by a term closely associated with it.

> *crown* [for king], *sail* [for ship], *The kettle is boiling* [for The water in the kettle is boiling; or for The situation is coming to a head].

(5) *Personification:* a form of metaphor infrequently used in modern writing, which attributes human qualities to objects or ideas.

> With how sad steps, O Moon, thou climb'st the skies!
> How silently, and with how wan a face.

> Duty commanded and he obeyed.

b. Appropriate figurative language serves to make expression concrete and vivid.

c. Trite figures of speech should be avoided.

> **Trite similes:** *pretty as a picture, happy as a lark, fresh as a daisy.*
> **Trite metaphors:** *budding genius, crack of dawn, lap of luxury.*
> **Trite personifications:** *Father Time, Mother Nature.*

d. Mixed, or awkwardly combined, figures of speech should be avoided.

> The *odor* of magnolias *shouted* a welcome.
> In the argument he *brought his big guns* into play and *stifled* his opponent.
> While he was courageously *battling* his way *through the sea of life, fate stepped in and tripped him up.*

e. Strained and inappropriate figures of speech should be avoided.

> Trees were dressed in their best bibs and tuckers preparing for their farewell-to-summer ball.
> Her smile was as warm as an electric heater.

24. GOOD PARAGRAPHS ¶

a. A good paragraph in expository writing usually has a clear topic sentence or topic idea, which gives unity to the paragraph.

b. A good paragraph has coherent arrangement of material and clear transitions between sentences. (See "Transitions," page 66.)

c. Good paragraphs begin and end strongly.

d. Paragraphs in a paper should be linked to one another by transitions that make the organization evident to the reader. (See "Transitions," page 66.)

e. As a rough guide to paragraph length, the student should bear in mind that paragraphs in expository writing rarely exceed 300 words and rarely fall below 100.

f. Good paragraphs are usually concrete and fully developed.

g. Eight ways of organizing paragraphs, often used in combination, are:
   (1) chronological arrangement
   (2) general-to-particular or particular-to-general arrangement
   (3) analysis
   (4) contrast and comparison
   (5) definition
   (6) cause and effect
   (7) reasons
   (8) question to answer or problem to solution

h. The first and last paragraphs in a paper occupy positions of greatest emphasis, and should be written with particular care.

25. INTEREST Int

Since human beings are interested in very different things, the techniques of being interesting differ with audience and circumstances. Student writing is likely to be most interesting when the student chooses a subject in which he himself is interested, and when he writes with the needs and interests of an audience in mind. He will then ask himself such questions as: What is my audience probably interested in? How much information about this topic do they probably have? At what points might they be puzzled and lose interest unless I explain more fully? How can I cause them to share my interest in this material?

One answer to the last question is: Be concrete. Use words, facts, examples, concrete comparisons, and details to stir the mind and senses of the audience and enable them to share the writer's knowledge and experience.

If passages in a composition are marked **int** (lacking in interest), the writer should examine them to see if the ideas are abstract and underdeveloped—if he has failed to set down on paper the concrete particulars needed to make the material interesting. It is also possible that the writing lacks interest because the writer is stating the obvious, because he is giving evidence of no real thought about the subject, or because his sentences are monotonously unvaried.

26. LEVELS OF USAGE — Lev

The term *levels of usage* refers to varieties of English: the differences in construction, pronunciation, and vocabulary produced by differences in education and in economic and social circumstances. Although the varieties are shifting and overlapping, it is possible to point out certain characteristics of each. Nonstandard English, used by people with little or no education, is nearly always spoken, seldom written except in fiction that reproduces this type of speech. It has numerous words and structures in common with standard English, but it is characterized by misuse of words, use of nonstandard words, and the corruption of what is now considered correct or conventional grammatical form. The three main varieties of standard English are formal English, informal English, and colloquial English. Formal English, more often written than spoken, is used by highly educated people in formal situations. Among its characteristics are long sentences, often in parallel and balanced constructions; impersonal style; and a wide and exact vocabulary. Informal English is the English most commonly written and spoken by educated people. Colloquial English is conversational English, more often spoken than written, which has the short sentences and the casual constructions and vocabulary of the everyday, relaxed speech of educated people.

a. Usage (formal, informal, or colloquial) should be appropriate to the subject, the audience, and the occasion.

b. Unless there is a positive gain in a shift, usage should be consistent in a passage or a composition.

c. Students should aim at high informal English in most of their writing.

d. In high informal writing, slang is usually out of place.

e. "Heavy" words, over-formal and pretentious for their context, should be avoided.

27. PARALLELISM — Par, ||

Parallelism is the principle of usage which requires that coordinate elements

in a compound construction be given the same grammatical form. Words, phrases, clauses, and even sentences may be put in parallel form.

a. Faulty parallelism occurs when logically coordinate elements are not expressed in parallel form.

> FAULTY: He is afraid to live and of death.
> PARALLEL: He is afraid to live and to die. [*Or*] He is afraid of life and of death.
>
> FAULTY: The mayor promised that he would build new sidewalks, provide new equipment for the schools, and reducing the taxes.
> PARALLEL: The mayor promised that he would build new sidewalks, provide new equipment for the schools, and reduce the taxes. [Three verbs.] [*Or*] The mayor promised to build new sidewalks, to provide new equipment for the schools, and to reduce the taxes. [Three infinitives.] [*Or*] The mayor promised new sidewalks, new equipment for the schools, and reduced taxes. [Three nouns.]

b. Faulty parallelism occurs when elements not logically coordinate are expressed in parallel form.

> FAULTY: He is tall, thin, and a Sigma Chi.
> LOGICAL: He is a tall, thin Sigma Chi.
>
> FAULTY: The teacher said Maynard was lazy, careless, and had better get to work.
> LOGICAL: The teacher said that Maynard was lazy and careless, and that he had better get to work.

28. REPETITION   Rep

a. Awkward and unnecessary repetition of words and sounds should be avoided.

> AWKWARD: The *fact* is, I *do* my best *writing* when *doing factual writing*.
> IMPROVED: I write best when I deal with facts.
>
> AWKWARD: The *shipper* checks the *merchandise* which has been *shipped* in, then the *shipper* puts the *merchandise* into stock.
> IMPROVED: The shipper checks the merchandise as it comes in and then puts it into stock.

b. Skillful repetition is an element of style, used for clarity and emphasis.

> The only thing we have to *fear* is *fear* itself . . .
> *We shall fight* on the beaches, *we shall fight* on the landing grounds, *we shall fight* in the fields and in the streets, *we shall fight* in the hills . . .

29. SUBORDINATION   Sub

Subordination means expressing in dependent clauses, or phrases, or single

words, ideas not important enough to be expressed in main clauses or independent sentences.

a. **Subordination is used to avoid:**
   (1) Choppy "primer" sentences:

   CHOPPY: I have a teacher named Mr. Mulch. He teaches biology. He is very strict.
   IMPROVED BY SUBORDINATION: Mr. Mulch, my biology teacher, is very strict.

   (2) Sprawling "and-and" sentences:

   SPRAWLING: The bell rings and he comes into class, and he takes attendance.
   IMPROVED BY SUBORDINATION: As soon as the bell rings, he comes into class and takes attendance.

b. **When subordination is used effectively, less important ideas are usually placed in subordinate constructions, and important ideas are expressed emphatically in independent clauses.**

   LACK OF SUBORDINATION (equal emphasis to ideas not equally significant): I was stepping off the curb and the truck hit me.
   UPSIDE-DOWN SUBORDINATION: (emphasis on the less significant idea): When the truck hit me, I was stepping off the curb.
   PROPER EMPHASIS ON THE MORE SIGNIFICANT IDEA: As I was stepping off the curb, the truck hit me.

c. **An awkward series of subordinate clauses in a sentence should be avoided.**

   AWKWARD: He is the man who has bought the Nelsons' house for which he paid twenty thousand dollars which he borrowed from his brother-in-law.
   IMPROVED: He borrowed twenty thousand dollars from his brother-in-law to buy the Nelsons' house.

d. **Subordinating conjunctions should be grammatically correct and should express clearly the relationship between ideas.**

   POOR: He doesn't know *as* he can take the courses he wants.
   REVISED: He doesn't know *that* (or *whether*) he can take the courses he wants.

   POOR: *Whereas* Edward needs money, he is looking for a part-time job.
   REVISED: *Because* Edward needs money, he is looking for a part-time job.

   POOR: I read in the book *where* paragraphs should have topic sentences.
   REVISED: I read in the book *that* paragraphs should have topic sentences.

   For further discussion of the use of connectives, see "Connectives," page 36.

30. TONE

Tone is the manner of verbal expression that a speaker or writer adopts. It reveals his attitudes, chiefly attitudes toward his audience and himself.

When passages in a student composition are marked for tone, the writer should examine them, perhaps read them aloud, to see if he has unintentionally been dogmatic, aggressive, pompous, or condescending; or if he has been inappropriately familiar, emotional, or sarcastic.

31. TRANSITIONS   Trans

Transitions are words, phrases, sentences, or even paragraphs, which show the reader the connections between the writer's ideas.

a. Transitions between sentences within a paragraph are established by:

(1) Using sentence connectives such as *therefore, however, on the other hand, consequently, at the same time.*

(2) Repeating a key word that has occurred in the preceding sentence, or using a term clearly equivalent to a term in the preceding sentence or a term clearly in contrast to one in the preceding material.

(3) Using a clear pronoun reference to a word or idea in the preceding sentence.

(4) Putting parallel thoughts in parallel constructions to show the relationships between them.

(5) Using subordination and subordinating conjunctions to clarify the relationships between important and less important ideas.

b. Transitions between paragraphs are established by:

(1) Concluding a paragraph with a sentence that leads into the next paragraph.

(2) Using in the first sentence of a paragraph a transitional word or phrase: *furthermore, as a result, in addition, on the contrary.*

(3) Repeating a key word used in the preceding paragraph.

(4) Beginning a paragraph with a sentence that refers clearly to a statement at the end of the preceding paragraph or to its topic idea.

(5) Using short transitional paragraphs to summarize the preceding ideas and relate them to the idea that follows.

32. UNITY AND FOCUS

A composition, a paragraph, or a sentence has unity and focus when it has a dominant idea to which all details within the unit are clearly relevant.

The fault of disunity in sentences is most commonly produced by (1) including material which is irrelevant or which appears to be irrelevant because of the absence of subordination or connectives, and (2) joining in one sentence apparently unrelated ideas, or too many ideas.

> LACK OF UNITY: I have come to this college, which will be a hundred years old next year, to study business administration. [The age of the college is irrelevant to the main idea of the sentence.]
> IMPROVED: I have come to this college to study business administration.
>
> LACK OF UNITY: Charles Dickens wrote *Martin Chuzzlewit* in 1843, and I enjoyed it a great deal. [Two very different ideas are faultily joined in one sentence.]
> IMPROVED: Charles Dickens wrote his enjoyable novel *Martin Chuzzlewit* in 1843.
>
> LACK OF UNITY: Helen had always been afraid of the dark and now she was fifteen years old. [The two ideas seem wholly unrelated.]
> IMPROVED: For as many of her fifteen years as she could remember, Helen had been afraid of the dark.
>
> LACK OF UNITY: Children in grade school are likely to regard their teachers as gods, or sometimes as tyrants, and then later they realize that teachers are human and can be advisers and friends, and they change their attitudes, which is something I did rather late, but which I have done now. [This sprawling, overloaded sentence contains too many ideas for one sentence.]
> IMPROVED: Children in grade school usually think of their teachers as gods or tyrants. Later, students realize that teachers are human beings who can be advisers and friends. I have arrived, rather tardily, at this more mature attitude toward my teachers.

Unity is closely related to coherence, emphasis, subordination, and the use of exact connectives. For further information about particular aspects of unity, see "Connectives," page 36, "Faulty Relationships of Sentence Elements," page 51, "Coherence," page 57, "Emphasis," page 59, "Subordination," page 64, and "Transitions," page 66.

Focus in a paper is achieved when the writer aims consistently, with a specific purpose, at a central subject. Focus requires the omission of extraneous matter, and the proportionate development of major and minor parts of the material.

33. VARIETY   Monot, Var

a. Monotonous repetition of words, sounds, and sentence structures should be avoided.

MONOTONOUS REPETITION: My general reaction to his action was that in general he acted wisely.
IMPROVED: I felt that in general he acted wisely.

MONOTONOUS CHOPPY SENTENCES: Joan came into the house. It was dark. The clock was striking seven.
IMPROVED: When Joan came into the dark house, the clock was striking seven.

MONOTONOUS SENTENCE PATTERNS: Having had a hard day at the office, Joe lost his temper quickly. Recovering from his anger, he regretted what he had said. Knowing that he was sorry, Martha accepted his apology.
IMPROVED: Joe, after a hard day at the office, lost his temper quickly. As soon as he recovered from his anger, he regretted what he had said, and Martha, knowing that he was sorry, accepted his apology.

b. Variety in sentence movement is achieved by:

(1) Varying the length of sentences.

(2) Using parallel and balanced constructions as a change from simpler constructions.

(3) Intermingling loose and periodic sentences.

(4) Changing the position of modifiers and parenthetic elements.

(5) Changing the subject-verb-object order of some sentences.

Sentence variety is closely related to subordination and to emphasis: in varying the movement of his sentences, the writer must consider what ideas he wants to emphasize by structure and position.

HANDBOOK

Section 4

PUNCTUATION

Punctuation rules are simply ways of stating the generally accepted, conventional meaning of punctuation marks. The able writer is aware of the important part such marks play in clarifying meaning and giving emphasis, and he departs from the conventions only when there is clear and positive advantage to be gained from doing so.

34. APOSTROPHE (') — Apos

a. The apostrophe is used to indicate the possessive case of nouns and of indefinite pronouns (*everyone's, everybody's, someone's, somebody's*, etc.). **The apostrophe is NOT used to form the possessive case of personal pronouns** (*his, hers, its, ours, yours, theirs*) or of the pronoun *who* (*whose*).

(1) To form the possessive of singular and plural nouns not ending in *s* or an *s* sound, use the apostrophe plus *s*.

    Tom's shoes   day's work   man's fate   men's clothes
    sons-in-law's hats   anybody's coat   anybody else's coat

(2) To form the possessive of plural nouns ending in *s*, use the apostrophe alone.

    soldiers' uniforms   friends' houses   ladies' jewelry

(3) To form the possessive of singular nouns ending in *s* or in *s* sounds, use either the apostrophe alone, or the apostrophe plus *s*.

> Burns's [*Or*] Burns' poetry

b. The apostrophe plus *s* is used to form the plurals of letters, figures, and signs when the apostrophe is needed for clarity; otherwise *s* alone may be used.

> There are three *a*'s in Alaska.
> The little girl wrote *1*'s for *7*'s.
> He has learned his ABCs.

c. The apostrophe is used to indicate the omission of one or more letters or numbers.

> They won't come, and we can't meet without them.
> He said the 'gator [alligator] was dangerous.
> "Abner was goin' down the road 'bout twenty miles an hour," Uncle Ike said.
> Edna graduated in '66, and Marshall was in the class of '62.

EXERCISES

I. Insert the needed apostrophes in the following sentences:

1. There are two *r*s and two *i*s in Henrys last name.
2. She doesnt think its necessary to study.
3. That handwriting is either James or hers.
4. Its unlikely that hell arrive before eight oclock.
5. There were thirteen *and*s, eight *but*s and three *so*s in the first page of the theme.

II. Write the contractions for the following expressions; if no recognized contracted form exists, write *none*.

shall not	is not	she will
will not	can not	he will
would not	must not	it is
could not	should not	they are
are not	may not	we have
am not	might not	it has

III. Write the possessive singular and, if it exists, the possessive plural of each of the following:

COLON

she	man	army
it	woman	NLRB
he	child	country
one	president	fox
you	James	D.A.R.
I	Henry	lady

35. BRACKETS ([ ])

Brackets are most commonly used to enclose interpolations by the writer or the editor in quoted material.

"He [Calvin Coolidge] had the reputation of being a man of few words."
"That year [1860] he met Lincoln for the first time."
The little boy wrote, "I didn't mispell [*sic*] any words today."

Brackets may be used, as they are used in this book, to enclose comments on illustrative material. They also serve as parentheses within parentheses.

36. COLON (:)

The colon is a formal and specialized mark indicating introduction, anticipation, or amplification.

a. The colon is used to introduce a formal quotation or a formal listing of particulars.

In his speech of July 3, 1970, Senator Patwell said: "This un-American law . . ."
The college library has ordered the following books: . . .
The villagers showed their fear of the new machine: the women averted their eyes, the children became silent, and the men muttered uneasily to one another.

b. The colon is used to follow the salutation of a business letter.

Dear Sir: Dear Mr. Nelson: Gentlemen:

c. The colon is used to separate: hours from minutes (12:15), a title from a subtitle (*The English Romantic Poets: A Review of Research*), and chapter from verse (John 3:3).

EXERCISES

Insert or substitute brackets and colons where they are needed in the following business letter; remove them where they are not needed, and supply the correct punctuation. If you are uncertain in choosing between brackets and parentheses see the discussion of parentheses on page 83.

> 801 Oregon Street
> Urbana, Illinois 61801
> January 2, 1972

Mr. Harold Mason, President
The Cornwall Company
56 Fifth Avenue
New York, N.Y. 10003

DEAR MR. MASON;

I am mailing to you today the following material: Chapters I, III, and V of Section One: Chapters II and IV of Section Two: and Chapters I and II of Section Three.

Your suggestions about: margins, numbering of pages, and use of headings are very helpful: they will solve some troublesome problems.

The two sentences that you were puzzled by [page 144, lines 8–12] do need revision. Below are the sentences as they originally were along with the changes that should be made;

Charles Fremont, grandson of Joclyn (should be Jocelyn) was born in Carecus (should be Caracas), Venezuela, on March 6 (should be March 8) at 8:29 A.M. His twin brother and loyal follower was born three hours later.

Please thank Mr. Edmonds for the research he has done and for his patience in reading the manuscript. My wife [who is doing the typing and who insists that my handwriting is illegible] also wants to thank Mr. Edmonds.

I hope to be able to send you the additions to Chapter VI of Section Two in a few days.

> Cordially yours,
> MARTIN S. BARRETT

37. COMMA (,)   C

The comma is the most frequently used mark of punctuation. Misuse of it produces not only mechanical errors, but also uncertainty and misunderstanding. A single comma is used to indicate a separation and a pause; commas in pairs are used to set off matter that constitutes some kind of additional unit but that does not need to be marked off by the longer and more emphatic pauses that would be indicated by a pair of dashes.

a. The comma is used to separate two independent clauses joined by *and, but, for, or,* or *nor.*

He promised to be here at six, but I don't expect him until seven.

Some handbooks on writing have stated this rule without qualification. Actually, the comma between independent clauses is often omitted, particularly if the clauses are not long. The comma after *six* is unnecessary in the sentence just cited; the sentence is perfectly clear without it. There is, however, a reason for this convention of using the comma between independent clauses joined by *and, but, for, or,* or *nor*:[1] frequently the subject of the second clause can momentarily be misread as the object of the first clause or the object of the preposition *for*. In the following sentences, commas are needed between clauses to prevent temporary misreading:

> I did not have time to buy the gift for Father hurried me away. [One naturally reads *gift for Father*.]
> I went to the railroad station to meet Mary and Frances went to the bus depot. [One reads *to meet Mary and Frances*.]
> I must call for the doctor said to let him know. [One reads *call for the doctor*.]

Because such temporary confusion can easily occur, many teachers insist that their students follow the rule and always use a comma between independent clauses joined by *and, but, for, or,* or *nor*. Certainly that conventional usage is safe. The student who takes liberties with it should be sure that he is not causing his reader the annoyance of stumbling over an unclearly punctuated sentence.

b. A comma should NOT be used to separate two independent clauses which are NOT joined by *and, but, for, or,* or *nor*. The use of a comma under these circumstances, when a semicolon or a period is needed, is called a **Comma Fault**, and a sentence so punctuated is called a **Run-together Sentence**. For a full discussion of the Comma Fault, see "Fused and Run-together Sentences," page 45.

c. The comma is generally used after an adverbial clause, a participial phrase, or any long phrase preceding the main part of the sentence.

> Since I gave you my promise, I will be there.

Here, and in many other sentences of similar pattern, the comma after the introductory clause or phrase is not really necessary. But it is generally advisable to follow this rule of punctuation, or at least to be aware of it, for two reasons: first, there is a natural pause for emphasis before a main clause that begins in the middle of a sentence, and the comma marks that emphatic pause; second, the omission of the comma, like the omission of the comma between main clauses, frequently produces misreading. Commas are confusingly omitted in the following sentences, even though some of the introductory clauses and phrases are short:

---

[1] Note that the comma *precedes* the conjunction.

> While he was riding his horse lost a shoe.
> After all I had done my best to help him.
> By testing emotional reactions are determined.
> To one who is interested in farming land has beauty and character.

On the whole, it is easier to follow the convention of using the comma to set off the introductory clause or phrase than it is to examine each sentence to be sure that it is immediately clear. The use of the comma in this situation is never "wrong." The omission of it may be troublesome, because it may cause the reader to go back and to supply for himself the pause for clarity that should have been indicated by the writer.

Sometimes, as we have suggested, the comma after introductory expressions is used less for clarity than for the pause and emphasis that would occur in speech and in thought. The following sentences illustrate:

> Smiling shyly, she turned to go.
> Without waiting for his hostess to pick up her fork, Alan attacked the roast beef.
> Surprised at the good behavior of the large crowd, the police were helpful and friendly.

d. Commas are used to set off nonrestrictive modifiers; commas should not be used to set off restrictive modifiers.

> Charles Smith, who is ten years old, should know better than to throw stones. [Nonrestrictive modifier]
> People who live in glass houses shouldn't throw stones. [Restrictive modifier]

This conventional rule of punctuation is deeply rooted in common sense and logic. A restrictive modifier *identifies* or *restricts* the meaning of the word it modifies. It is not set off by commas because it is an essential part of the context and is necessary to fix or limit the meaning of the word:

> Students who are failing any course are requested to see the Dean. [*Who are failing any course* is a restrictive clause; it identifies the students requested to see the Dean.]

A nonrestrictive modifier gives *additional* information about an *already identified* subject. It is set off by commas because it is simply a parenthetical element or a conveyor of fact supplementary, not essential, to the main point of the sentence:

> My oldest sister, who married a British sailor, is visiting us. [*Oldest* clearly identifies the sister; hence, *who married a British sailor* is clearly a nonrestrictive modifier.]

Confusion or distortion of meaning may result from the illogical punctuation of restrictive and nonrestrictive modifiers. Consider the difference in meaning in the following sentences:

All our money, which we had left on the beach, was taken by the thief.
All our money which we had left on the beach was taken by the thief.
[In the first sentence the loss is apparently more serious: all our money was taken. In the second sentence, only the money which we had left on the beach was taken. The writer who has had three dollars stolen while he was swimming is probably giving misinformation if he records his loss in the form of the first sentence.]

The members of the football team, who ate at the hotel, have ptomaine poisoning.
The members of the football team who ate at the hotel have ptomaine poisoning.
[The coach would be more distressed by the situation represented in the first sentence.]

The examples of restrictive and nonrestrictive modifiers that we have been considering are clauses. In the sentences below, phrases give additional information about an identified subject; these nonrestrictive phrases are properly set off by commas:

Mary, now tired, returned to work.
Mother, concerned at the lateness of the hour, was awake when I came home.
Professor Greenleaf, having failed to hear the bell, talked on.

The logical punctuation of restrictive and nonrestrictive modifiers can usually be determined by reading the sentence aloud. If the modifier is naturally set off with pauses when one reads, it should be set off by commas in the written sentence.

e. Commas are used to set off words, phrases, or clauses that are thrown in as interrupters or parenthetical elements when the grammatical structure is complete without them.

He is, however, unwilling to accept the compromise.
War and unemployment, on the other hand, are ever-present dangers.
He, it is said, was more to blame than his son.

f. Commas are used to separate elements (words, phrases, or clauses) in a series.

Papers were strewn on the table, on the desk, and on the floor.
He enjoys hunting, fishing, and swimming.
He stated that conflict was imminent, that the opponents were well prepared, and that he felt uncertain of victory.
He was tired, he was hungry, and he was very late.

(When there is no danger of ambiguity or misreading, it is permissible to omit the comma before the final element in the series.)

g. Commas are used to set off a nonrestrictive appositive. (An appositive is a noun or a noun equivalent used to explain another noun construction which has the same referent.)

>Mr. Morgan, John's father, was pleased. [Nonrestrictive appositive; commas are needed.]
>The poet Milton was blind. [Restrictive appositive; commas should not be used.]

h. Commas are used to separate coordinate adjectives not joined by a conjunction.

>The tall, thin man shrugged his shoulders.
>We watched the dawn of a bleak, wintry day.
>The long, hot, difficult journey was nearly over.

The comma is *not* used when adjectives in series are not coordinate. In the sentences above, each adjective seems to modify the noun directly. In other series, each adjective modifies a complex of adjectives and noun. Examples are:

>They live in a red brick house. [Here *red* modifies the locution *brick house; red* and *brick* are not coordinate.]
>The tired old man staggered under the load. [*Tired* modifies *old man*.]
>The beautiful little blond dog was waiting at the door. [Here, each adjective modifies the whole expression that follows.]

i. Commas are used to set off nouns of address.

A noun of address, which names the person or persons spoken to, may be a sentence interrupter; but it may also be at the beginning or end of a sentence:

>Now, Jake, you know how it is.
>I appreciate your advice, Doctor, but I cannot follow it.
>Sir, may I change the time of my conference?
>Let us consider carefully, my friends.

j. Commas are used to set off a short direct quotation from the rest of the sentence.

>"All these people," she said, "are strangers to me."
>He said, "Are you going now?"
>"You must go now," he said.

k. A comma is used to separate the parts of dates, addresses, and geographical names.

>On August 17, 1967, his address was 14 Barton Street, Peoria, Illinois; later he moved to Cleveland, Ohio, to live near his sister. [But Zip Code numbers are not separated: Medford, Massachusetts 02155.]

l. A comma is generally used to set off a brief introductory expression.

Yes, I know what you mean.
Well, that's what he said.
No, Vivian is not practical.
Oh, I'm sorry to hear this.
In short, he was a remarkable man.

m. A comma is used to prevent misreading. (Sometimes the fact that commas are needed to prevent misreading is a hint that the sentence needs to be revised.)

Before, he had insisted on cash payment.
For him, to buy was better than to sell.

n. Commas are used (1) when they are needed to clarify meaning by marking a slight pause, and (2) when they are required by some of the established conventions stated in the rules above. Commas that are not justified by (1) or (2) should be omitted.

Commas should *not* be used to separate words that form an organic unit in the sentence; they should *not* separate a subject from its verb in a simple sentence, a verb from its object, an adjective from its noun, or a conjunction from the clause it introduces. The following examples illustrate a haphazard misuse of commas: the commas clutter the sentences, creating pauses where no pauses should occur.

Gay streamers and floating balloons, decorated the gymnasium.
The way to success, is often, a long and difficult, road.
Mother said, she disapproved of the plan.
I refuse to go unless, you go with me.
The angry, members of the committee, protested loudly, but, the chairman was firm.

The organic and therefore proper use of commas can often, as in these sentences, be determined by reading the sentence aloud. Unless a comma is demanded by some well-established convention, it should be used only when a slight pause is natural, or is needed for clarity or emphasis.

EXERCISES

I. Decide whether to use commas, semicolons, or no mark of punctuation in the places where there is a caret ($\wedge$) in the sentences below, and cite the rule that applies. (Before you do this exercise, see rules **a** and **b** under "Semicolon," page 90.)

1. The wind is blowing$\wedge$ but the sun is warm.
2. "I am willing$\wedge$" he said$\wedge$ "to give money to such a cause$\wedge$ and I do not want my name used in connection with it."

3. He was old∧ he was tired∧ and he was unwilling to learn new ways.
4. In the winter∧ there is snow to shovel∧ in the summer∧ there is grass to cut∧ in the fall∧ there are leaves to rake∧ only in the early spring is there leisure.
5. We waited at home until she returned∧ for Mother was worried about her∧ and Father was worried about the car.
6. He said∧ "My children are sick∧ my wife is ill∧ and I have no money."
7. The Arnolds brought ice, lemonade, and cookies∧ the Lanes brought frankfurts∧ rolls, and wood for the fire∧ and we brought potato salad, oranges, and a large thermos jug full of coffee.
8. Maynard gets sleepy as soon as he opens his chemistry book∧ he can read a detective story∧ though∧ until three in the morning.
9. Speech is silver∧ silence is golden.
10. If you ask him a question∧ he does not answer∧ if you tell him something∧ he forgets it immediately.
11. The driver slowed down∧ when he saw the police car∧ then he turned sharply into a country lane∧ and roared away.
12. He is very polite∧ in fact, he is too polite∧ and I distrust him.

II. In the sentences below, the expressions in italics are restrictive or nonrestrictive modifiers. Insert commas wherever they are needed for proper punctuation of these modifiers.

1. Marcella *who is very sensitive* often has her feelings hurt.
2. His hair *gray and sparse* made him look older than he actually was.
3. The men *who were the fathers of the American Revolution* would be surprised at the actions of some of their descendants.
4. He admits that history *which he calls his least interesting subject* is the course for which he studies least.
5. The subjects *which Edward likes best* are psychology and anthropology.
6. Tom *startled by the sudden question and only half awake* mumbled a reply and went to sleep again.
7. His latest book *on which he worked for seven years* is said to be inferior to his earlier books.
8. The sun *obscured by the cloud of smoke* cast a ray of light on the path ahead of us.
9. We saw our friend *still smiling and serene* open the door to the Dean's office.
10. Martin *who has never read a book in his life* says that he hopes to be a newspaper man and a critic.

III. Correct or revise all sentences in which commas are omitted or misused.

1. She asked for Fred and Mark and Walter felt slighted.
2. The birds disturbed Henrietta, sometimes, they woke her up just before dawn.
3. The address of the tall, thin, man is 12 Fifth Avenue, New York, New York, 10003.
4. "If I come to dinner," she said, "I'll have to bring my father who is visiting me, and a friend, who is visiting him."

5. He had to work hard for the firm of Hamilton, Cook, and Boggle makes heavy demands on the people, whom it employs.
6. I have swallowed too much salt and sand is in my hair.
7. I waited forty minutes for Betty and Joan are always late.
8. As I expected the invitation to the wedding came this morning.
9. Children, who are public nuisances, should be kept at home.
10. The play lasted for three hours, however the audience liked it.
11. No I cannot help you Hubert my friend.
12. Paul who is not concerned about his appearance, likes to wear comfortable, old clothes.
13. Professor I'd like to talk with you, if I could sometime about an exciting short story I read last night.
14. Irene's youngest brother Ned who has been in Vietnam for a year is back at home.
15. Everyone who was invited was there but Elsie a small slender girl, with red hair, had to leave early.

IV. In the passage below strike out any commas that are not *required* according to the conventions of punctuation.

Polly said, "It's too small, for a wedding announcement," and tore open the letter, as Jim went out to bring in the rest of the groceries, from the car. Below him, as he walked down, the steps of the cottage, the lake shimmered blue in the noonday sun. There were no more bundles in the car, and he slammed the door, listening to the sharp, crack in the clear, air. Everything was intensified like that here: sound and smell and color, and the sensations of sunlight and used muscles and refreshment after sleep. He sat down on the low, flat, boulder, at the meeting of the two paths, one zigzagging from the cottage down to the beach, the other winding up to the knoll with its single crooked, pine tree, overlooking the lake. The stone was warm from the sun. With the side of his shoe, he scraped together a pile of brown, pine needles, which covered the ground at his feet.

Polly came out on the porch. "Jim, Berda's in Boston and wants to come up this week-end. We haven't invited anyone else, have we?"

"I haven't." He grinned at his sister, over his shoulder. "How about your wide-eyed medical friends?"

"They can't come. And they are not wide-eyed," she added, good-naturedly.

38. DASH (—)

The dash, skillfully used, does much to clarify meaning; unskillfully used, it misleads the reader and suggests that the writer is using punctuation to suit his own convenience rather than to guide the reader. Dashes may be used singly or in pairs.

a. Dashes are used in pairs to set off interpolations to which the writer wishes to give greater emphasis than parentheses or commas would give them.

He said—you can imagine how this pleased me—that he would not accept my handwritten paper.

These three elements—fact, attitude, and intention—combine to produce the compound of meaning.

Charles, you must—don't scuff your feet and wear out your shoes—you must return Mr. Hazlitt's rake.

b. A single dash is used to mark an unexpected turn of thought, an abrupt suspension of sense, a sudden change in structure or a hesitation in speech.

He gave a—I'm sorry; I promised not to tell.

Beets, carrots, tomatoes, corn, chard, onions—all these I planted in the unfertile soil. At the end of the summer I had well-fed worms and a flourishing crop of—weeds!

Mary heard Tom say to her father, "Mr. Hodge, I—that is, we—well—uh—Mary said—to ask . . . ."

c. The dash should not be carelessly used as a substitute for other marks of punctuation.

(In general the dash serves as a signal that either the substance or the construction of the material it sets off demands particular attention. In typing, the dash is made by combining two hyphens.)

39. ELLIPSIS (. . .)

Ellipsis is used to indicate the omission of a word or words needed to complete a sentence, or the omission of part of a quotation. The ellipsis consists of three spaced periods.

Four periods instead of three are used in an ellipsis if it comes at the end of a sentence which is closed by a period, or if a period occurs in the material omitted.

I know that I should do it, but . . . .

Newman says that a university education "gives a man a clear conscious view of his own opinions and judgments, . . . an eloquence in expressing them, and a force in urging them."

40. EXCLAMATION POINT (!)

The exclamation point is used after an ejaculation (word, phrase, or entire sentence) to indicate emphatic utterance or strong feeling.

Ouch!   Get out!   And we spent our youth learning grammar!

Overuse of exclamation points can suggest that a writer is gushing or insincere:

> It was her first dance! She was going with Ted! Wonderful Ted! And he had sent her a corsage! A corsage of white roses!
>
> Her husband has bought her a Whiz vacuum cleaner! Now she knows he loves her! Now housework will be thrilling!

41. HYPHEN (-)

The hyphen is used primarily to show close relationships between words or parts of words.

a. The hyphen is used at the end of a line when part of a word is carried over to the next line. (See "Syllabification," page 108.)

b. Hyphens are used in the writing of certain compound expressions.

Rules for the writing of compound words are not completely fixed, and authorities differ about the use of a hyphen in particular cases. Some compounds (especially those that have been long and frequently used) are written as one word *(nevertheless)*, other compounds are hyphenated *(ex-president)*, and still others are written as separate words *(commander in chief)*. Hyphens should always be used when they are necessary for clarity; for example, *a wooden-shoe maker* and *a wooden shoemaker* have different meanings. Although a writer often has an option of using or not using a hyphen, after he has made his choice he should be consistent. The best source of information about hyphens in particular expressions is a good modern dictionary.

Common practice calls for the use of hyphens:

(1) in compound numbers from twenty to one hundred and in the writing of fractions.

> twenty-one, twenty-first [*but*] one hundred and twenty-one and one hundred and twenty-first
>
> two-thirds, three one-hundredths, forty-two twenty-fifths

(2) between the letters of a spelled word, and to indicate the division of a word into syllables.

> *Already* is spelled a-l-r-e-a-d-y.
> *Athlete* has two syllables: ath-lete.

(3) in most compounds made up of nouns and prepositional phrases.

> hand-to-hand, eyeball-to-eyeball, mother-in-law, man-of-war

(4) between words which function as a single adjective before a substantive (noun or pronoun).

an off-the-face hat [*but*] off the face of the earth
a broken-down car [*but*] The car was broken down.
a hard-drinking man
a will-you-step-outside-with-me look

(5) in a word to differentiate it from another word spelled the same way.

re-cover and recover
re-creation and recreation

(6) in most words compounded with *self* or *ex* as a prefix.

self-conceit, self-reliance, self-pity [*but not in* selfless, selfsame]
ex-president, ex-senator, ex-convict, ex-wife

(7) in most compounds made up of prefixes joined to proper nouns.

anti-American, pro-Communist, pre-Raphaelite

(8) between two or more words that, though separated, modify the same noun.

differences between pre- and post-revolutionary China
using 2- by 6-inch boards

42. ITALICS   Ital, Und

Italics are indicated in manuscript by underlining the word or words to be italicized. Practice varies greatly in the use of italics by newspapers, magazines, and book publishers, and italics (i.e., underlining in manuscript) are more frequently used in formal than in colloquial or familiar writing. The following rules should be followed in formal or high informal writing.

a. Italics are used for titles of books, pamphlets, newspapers, magazines, musical compositions, works of art, plays, movies, and for names of ships and aircraft.

Green Mansions, MLA Style Sheet, Boston Globe (or Boston *Globe*), *Newsweek, Idylls of the King,* U.S.S. *Missouri* (or the *Missouri*)

b. Italics are generally used for foreign words and phrases that have not been absorbed into English.

The ambassador was *persona non grata.*
The detective said, *"Cherchez la femme."*

c. Italics are used to call attention to words as words, letters as letters, figures as figures.

PARENTHESES

freedom, a word with many meanings
a word spelled with four *s*'s
the 7's that look like *9*'s

d. Italics are sometimes used for emphasis. (But italics, like other mechanical devices for emphasis—capitalization, use of exclamation points—lose their effect unless they are used sparingly.)

I shall *never* consent. [But not: The baby *was* a *darling* and Jane couldn't *wait* to tell Doris how *cute* he was.]

e. Italics are used for the scientific names of genera, subgenera, species, and subspecies.

the genera *Quercus* and *Liriodendron*

43. PARENTHESES (( ))

Parentheses are used to set off material (definitions, additional information, asides, illustrative detail) which helps to clarify, but is not essential. (Such material is thrown in, as we say, parenthetically.)

She said (but of course we knew better) that she was younger than her husband.
When the boy from Kentucky asked for a *sack* of peanuts in Boston, the clerk was puzzled. (New Englanders use the word *bag*.)
When he first introduces the symbol of the lantern (page 13, paragraph 2) he is describing his boyhood experience.
The dash has the following uses: (1) to . . . , (2) to . . . , and (3) to . . . .
The gear shift (see Diagram A) is different in the 1970 models.

In a composition, the deletion of a word or phrase is indicated by drawing a line through it, *not* by enclosing it in parentheses.

Except in business and legal usage, it is not customary to repeat a sum previously stated in words:

Legal or business usage: I enclose two hundred dollars ($200.00).
General usage: Here is a twenty-dollar check for your birthday.

When parenthetical material is at the end of an introductory clause or phrase that is to be set off by a comma from the rest of the sentence, the parenthetical element is *followed by*, not preceded by, the comma:

After Father had admonished me about driving carefully (as he often did), he delayed me further by asking me about my plans for the evening.
He said (I wondered why), "Do you expect to be going out again tomorrow?"
In the meantime (and it was a long time), the demonstrators had to content themselves with promises.

EXERCISES

I. State the main uses of each of the following marks of punctuation: dash, ellipsis, exclamation point, hyphen, italics, parentheses.

II. What is the difference in use between parentheses and brackets, between parentheses and dashes, between the hyphen and the dash? When are italics (or underlining) used in writing titles and when are quotation marks used? (See "Quotation Marks," page 87.)

III. In the sentences below examine the use of the dash, ellipsis, parentheses, and italics. In each case explain why that mark of punctuation is properly used or why it is misused. When you find a mark improperly used, strike it out and substitute whatever punctuation is necessary.

1. John Gunther's *Roosevelt in Retrospect* (New York: Harper & Brothers, 1950) was . . . or at least most reviewers seemed to think it was . . . a satisfactory treatment of a difficult subject.

2. Mr. Hamilton Basso, who wrote the review entitled *Another Go at F.D.R.* in "The New Yorker," expressed the following opinion: "Mr. Gunther . . . is one of the more uncritical of Roosevelt's admirers. He is in there all the time getting in his licks for his hero."

3. Several of the keys of her typewriter—the *a*, the *i*, the *l*, and the *g*—clearly need cleaning; also I wish that she would learn to spell "separate" properly.

4. Senator Rudland said he was going to his hotel (he pronounced it hó-tel) to get some sleep. Tomorrow he will sail for England on the *Queen Elizabeth*.

5. *Op. cit., loc. cit., passim, supra*—these Latin terms were once more widely used in footnotes than they now are.

IV. Supply hyphens where they are needed:

1. His down to earth statement surprised those who had expected a vague and fumbling answer from the eighty seven year old ex president.

2. His sister in law, a strong willed, self reliant woman, refused to wear high heeled shoes, insisted on continuing to wear her out of style hat, and was entirely satisfied with ankle length skirts.

3. We suspected that his never say die attitude was a pose and that his self confident air was equally misleading.

44. PERIOD (.)

a. **A period is used at the end of a sentence, or any expression standing for a sentence, that is neither interrogative nor exclamatory. The placing of a period after an unsatisfactory incomplete sentence produces the blunder known as the Period Fault.**

In the following examples the period is properly used:

Ralph was here today. [A complete declarative sentence.]
Go soon. [An imperative sentence; the subject *you* is understood.]
He asked where the fire was. [An indirect question.]
Will you please send me a copy of *Pilgrim's Progress*, cloth edition. [A request politely phrased as a question is often followed by a period.]
So much for the preparations. Now the next step. [In expository writing, transitional expressions which are not complete sentences may be punctuated as sentences.]
No. Can't stay any longer. See you tomorrow. [In the recording of spoken English, words or groups of words that stand for sentences are followed by a period.]
No movement of life in this desert. Only the glaring sun and the simmering waves of heat. [In narrative and descriptive writing, freer use is made of incomplete sentences.]

Ability to distinguish between acceptable and unacceptable incomplete sentences is essential to the proper use of the period. (See "Fragmentary and Incomplete Sentences," page 42.)

b. The period is used to make clear that a letter or a group of letters is an abbreviation of a longer locution. If a sentence ends with an abbreviation followed by a period, a second period is not needed.

U.S.A.   B.C.   Ph.D.   *ibid.*   i.e.   Dr. Holt   A.M. (or a.m.)
She lives in Boston, Mass.

(Certain abbreviations—UNRRA, UN, UNICEF, IOU—are written without periods. For information about particular abbreviations, consult your dictionary.)

c. The period is used to mark a decimal.

She paid $403.50 for the furniture she bought at the auction.
The cost of living has risen 60.42 per cent.

A series of periods, called *ellipsis*, is used to indicate the omission of a word or words necessary to complete a sentence, or the omission of a part of a quotation. (See "Ellipsis," page 80.)

EXERCISES

I. Define (1) complete sentence, (2) incomplete sentence, (3) fragmentary sentence. (If necessary see "Fragmentary and Incomplete Sentences," page 42.)

II. In the passages below (1) point out any fragmentary sentences and revise to eliminate the period fault, (2) point out any acceptable incomplete sentences and explain why you think they are acceptable, (3) point out the subject and the verb of each independent clause or sentence, and (4) add any periods that are needed and strike out any unnecessary periods.

1. He did not know the abbreviation for United States. Which is U.S.
2. We were pleased at the progress our club had made. Only a year, yet twenty-seven members now and $227.40 in our treasury.
3. We told the freshman to ring the chapel bell at two A.M. Which, much to our surprise, he did and woke up Dean Holden.
4. What would be a reasonable sum? Dick did not want to overpay the man, but he wanted to be fair. Perhaps thirty dollars. That seemed too much. Perhaps twenty-five or perhaps even twenty. Yes, twenty would do.
5. Henry was surprised to see Andy walking slowly ahead of him.
"Andy," he shouted, "Is that you, Andy?"
"Yeah." Andy's voice didn't sound friendly.
"Where are you going?"
"Just walking." Andy was waiting for him now under the light. His collar was turned up and he looked cold.
"I thought you were seeing Anne tonight."
"Yeah. I was."
"But it's only—"
"Only nine. That's right, and I'm not with Anne. Funny, isn't it. Well, I'll tell you . . ."
6. She was thinking. Of nothing at all. When suddenly the doorbell rang, she went to answer it.
7. He did very little studying. Although he was a member of the ROTC and needed to maintain a high average.
8. Everything he saw pleased him. The spacious campus. The ivy-covered buildings. The friendly students. He felt sure now that he would like college. Very much.
9. Bright sun. Blue sky. White sand. Mrs. Marlowe looked at the scene in amazement.
10. I received four dollars in tips. Thus making my income for the day $12.75.

45. QUESTION MARK (?)

The question mark is placed at the end of a direct question or is used parenthetically to express doubt.

When are you going? [A direct question.]
He asked when we were going. [An indirect question; no question mark is needed.]
He asked, "When are you going?"
Did he really say, "You will regret this"? [An interrogative sentence that contains a quoted statement.]
Did he actually say, "Why should I pay for food like this?" [A question that contains a quoted question.]

She says—can you believe it?—that she will be prompt.

Arnold promised to come, but can we really expect him? [A sentence beginning with a statement but ending with a question.]

Chaucer, born in 1342(?), anticipated the English Renaissance. [A parenthetical expression of doubt or uncertainty.]

Because punctuation of indirect questions sometimes poses a problem, it is well to emphasize that indirect questions are not followed by a question mark. The following examples are declarative sentences; the indirect questions embedded in the sentences are the objects of the verbs and are properly followed by periods.

I wondered if I should answer.
Neil asked himself what he should study first.
She inquired what the hurry was.
Many people have asked why we should go to Mars.

A question mark used to indicate humor or irony is often better omitted:

My father was glad to see his handsome(?) and intelligent(?) son.
The dancer innocently(?) cast off the sixth veil.

46. QUOTATION MARKS (" ") Quot

Quotation marks are used to enclose direct quotations and to call attention to locutions used in special ways.[2]

Single quotation marks (' ') are used within double quotation marks (" ") for a quotation within a quotation.

Quotation marks, whether single or double, are used before and after a locution to set it off. Careless omission of either the "before" or "after" mark is confusing to the reader.

In typed quotations, passages of two lines or more are usually single-spaced and indented from both margins. Quotation marks are then unnecessary. For long quotations which are not single-spaced or indented, a "before" or left-hand mark is placed at the beginning of each paragraph, but the "after" or right-hand mark is used only at the end of the last quoted paragraph, where it serves to indicate the end of the quoted material.

a. Quotation marks are used to enclose direct quotations.

The reporter wrote, "President De Gaulle did not say, 'We have faith in NATO'; he said, 'France must have a bomb of her own.'"

---

[2] Though printers and editors are in agreement about the use of quotation marks to indicate direct quotations, they are not in complete accord about special uses of quotation marks or about the position of other marks when quotation marks are used. The intent of this article and the following article is to indicate what appears to be the best practice for college students.

The first two lines of this poem are: "Thou still unravished bride of quietness,/ Thou foster child of silence and slow time."
Ned wrote home, "I don't much like the food or the discipline of the army."

b. Quotation marks are used to enclose locutions used in special ways:

(1) Titles of short poems, stories, magazine articles, and chapters of books. (Underlining—to indicate italics—is generally used for titles of books, magazines, newspapers, and plays.)

He read aloud parts of "To Autumn" and then gave a lecture on Keats.
He wrote a book report on Hardy's *The Return of the Native*.

(2) Technical terms that might confuse the reader if they were not identified as technical.

In the "lead" the reporter must give certain information.

(3) Expressions that the writer wishes to call attention to as words, sometimes for ironic effect. (In formal writing, such words are usually italicized, but they are commonly put in quotation marks in informal writing.)

"Recession" is a more pleasant word than "depression," and "strategic withdrawal" sounds better than "retreat."

c. Quotation marks should *not* be used to enclose indirect quotations or to excuse inappropriate phrasing:

WRONG: He said "that Tom will come."
POOR: Polonius was deceived because he did not know that Hamlet was "kidding him along."

47. QUOTATION MARKS WITH OTHER MARKS OF PUNCTUATION

a. Periods and commas are conventionally placed inside the close-quotation mark.

"It is difficult," Archibald said, "always to be in the right."
Richard, not understanding the word, was puzzled when his uncle talked about the importance of being a "gentleman."

Sometimes, as in the sentence just above, logic suggests putting a comma or a period outside the quotation mark. We are dealing here, however, not with logic but with convention, in this case a convention designed to make manuscript and printed pages neat and uniform. According to this convention, all commas and periods are put *inside* quotation marks.

b. Other punctuation marks should be placed inside the quotation marks only if they are part of the matter quoted.

"What do you mean?" he asked. [Since the quotation is a question, the question mark is inside the quotation marks.]

Can we ignore what Carl Becker called "the climate of opinion"? [The quotation is not a question; the question mark is therefore outside the quotation marks.]

"Stop!" she cried. [The quotation is an exclamation; the exclamation point is inside the quotation marks.]

"But I thought—" she began, then recalled her promise. [The dash is part of the quoted matter because it shows the abrupt halt in speech.]

He calls himself a "liberal"; what he means is not clear.

According to the defendant, these are the "facts": he was not in town on the night of the robbery, and he had honestly earned the money found on his person.

Semicolons and colons at the end of quoted material are almost never part of the quotation. These two marks of punctuation are, therefore, nearly always outside the quotation marks.

c. In quotations broken for identification of the speaker or for added detail, choice of other marks of punctuation depends on sentence structure.

"What I wonder," Janice said, "is how it can end." [The speech tag interrupts an unfinished sentence and so is set off by commas.]

"You can feel the air pollution today," Roger said. "It must be well above the safe level." [Here a period follows *said* because Roger's first sentence is complete.]

"What is it?" She looked closely at him. "Has something happened?" [Added detail is a complete sentence between the two quoted questions.]

EXERCISES

Use quotation marks or italics where they are needed in the following sentences. When italics are needed, underline the word which should be italicized. (For the use of italics see page 82.) When quotation marks are needed, be sure to place them properly before or after other marks.

1. Dean Warren said, When I heard that student say ain't got no and this here, I understood why he did not pass his freshman English course.

2. The professor read aloud Browning's My Last Duchess; then he asked his students to give their interpretation of the poem.

3. Was it General MacArthur who said, I shall return?

4. While I waited for Dr. Martin, I read an article in Time entitled Congress and the Russians.

5. The footnote in Arthur G. Kennedy's book English Usage reads as follows: See H. B. Allen, The Standard of Usage in Freshman Textbooks, English Journal, Vol. 24, 1935, pp. 564–571.

6. I am very tired, Alice said emphatically, of hearing him talk about what he calls his sensitivity.

7. Sam's short story was entitled Beyond the Generation Gap. He said that it was publishable; but he added, My teacher has the soul of a proofreader.

8. Can you help me understand, Eleanor said, exactly what Camus means by the absurd?

9. John recited his favorite lines from Macbeth: Methought I heard a voice cry, Sleep no more! Macbeth doth murder sleep!

10. In which poem, the teacher asked, in The Road Not Taken or in Stopping By Woods, do we find the line But I have promises to keep?

48. SEMICOLON (;)   Semi

The semicolon, though actually an easy mark of punctuation to master, is second only to the comma in producing faults in student writing. In general a semicolon indicates a shorter pause and a closer connection than a period, and a longer pause and a less close connection than a comma.

a. The semicolon is used to separate two independent clauses *not* joined by *and, but, for, or,* or *nor*.

> They had reached a stalemate; neither would give in.
> He was discouraged; life had disappointed him.
> He irritates me at times; nevertheless I like him.

NOTE 1.—Failure to follow this rule produces the error known as the run-together sentence. (See "Fused and Run-together Sentences," page 45.)

NOTE 2.—An exception to Rule a above is the punctuation of three or more independent clauses in series: He was tired, he was hungry, and he was very late.

b. The semicolon is used to separate coordinate clauses joined by *and, but, for, or,* or *nor* when one of the coordinate clauses contains commas. (This is always a safe rule; one need not follow it, however, when a comma will give the desired clarity and emphasis.)

> The French fought for liberty, equality, fraternity; and peace was a secondary consideration. [Here the semicolon is needed for clarity.]
> Charles, Tom, and Elliot came in late, and their father asked them where they had been. [Here the comma is certainly justifiable.]

c. The semicolon is used to separate items in a series when one of the items itself contains a comma. (This rule, too, is dependent on context. Oftentimes a comma will serve the purpose.)

> She ordered doughnuts, cookies, and pies from the bakery; ice cream, chocolate sauce, and sherbet from the drugstore; and balloons, horns, and cap pistols from the corner store.

EXERCISES

(Before doing these exercises read the treatment of fused and run-together sentences, page 45, as well as the rules for the use of the semicolon.)

SEMICOLON

I. State the subject and the verb of each independent clause in the sentences below; then insert or substitute semicolons where they are required by Rules **a, b,** and **c.** As you punctuate each sentence, indicate which rule you are following, and indicate also whether a period or a comma might be used in place of the semicolon.

1. He will go his way, she will go hers.
2. He placed the key in the lock, and then, very cautiously, he opened the door.
3. When he is happy, she is happy, when he suffers, she suffers with him.
4. At first the man seemed friendly, then he became angry and abusive.
5. I know that he will come, what I don't know is how long he will stay.
6. He had talked about a new car and he had dreamed about a new car, now he was going to own one.
7. Some people content themselves with wishes, others turn wishes into actualities.
8. Life is a comedy to those who think, a tragedy to those who feel.
9. Still they came, the old men, the women, the children, and the young lieutenant looked on, full of pity but unable to help.
10. He refused to help, although the food was there and he could easily have spared it.
11. He finished the report, then he went to bed and slept for fourteen hours.
12. It isn't that he means to be cruel, he simply doesn't understand boys of that age.
13. I'm sure that he's coming to the game, in fact I sold him a ticket just an hour ago.
14. Open the door and let him in, he's standing out there in the rain.
15. He was sleepy, he was tired, and he was very cold.

II. Which of the following are run-together sentences?

1. Although he was not cowardly, he valued his life and he was unwilling to risk it unnecessarily.
2. She knows he will be in later, that is all she will say.
3. He was in need of money, therefore he accepted the job eagerly.
4. At first he was conscientious, later he became very lax.
5. Yes, Mercedes told me she had dented my fender naturally I wasn't pleased.

HANDBOOK

Section 5

MECHANICS

49. SPELLING   Sp

Spelling is important because it is so often the first basis on which a writer is judged. Conventional spelling is probably the clearest example of an established procedure to which one must conform, not because nonconformity destroys the sense of the communication (a word is seldom so badly misspelled as to be unrecognizable) but simply because many readers respond unfavorably, with irritation, disrespect, and mistrust, to the writer who cannot spell.

An occasional misspelling, particularly of an uncommon word, is not a serious error. Conspicuously poor spelling is serious, however, because it suggests that the writer is unfamiliar with printed material, or unable to learn what most educated people learn without great difficulty, or both. Such errors as confusing *there* and *their, its* and *it's, quite* and *quiet,* and misspelling words like *receive, believe, tries, beginning,* which are spelled according to established rules, create an impression of illiteracy. To many people, spelling is an index to the writer's education and intelligence. Actually it is not a reliable index, but the fact remains that one is judged by the way he spells.

Good spelling requires attention, memory, and the use of the ear, the eye, and the hand. In learning to spell a word the student should first be sure he knows the meaning and has before him the accepted pronunciation, syllabification, and spelling of the word; a good dictionary supplies this information. Next he should pronounce the word to fix it in his auditory memory, look at it closely to fix it in his visual memory, check his visual memory by looking a second time at the word, and then write it twice to record it in his muscular memory and to see it in his own handwriting. If the word is not yet fixed in his mind, he may find it useful to try other memory (mnemonic) devices: for example, he can write *separate* as *sepArate,* emphasizing the trouble spot with the large A, or he can fix in his mind the fact that there is *a rat* in *separate;* or in learning to spell *receive,* he can note that it follows the *ei-after-c* rule.

The student whose spelling is weak should not take the attitude that poor spelling is an incurable affliction to which he should be stoically—or even worse, cheerfully—resigned. Our experience leads us to believe that any college student (except for the very rare individuals who have special visual or psychological handicaps—perhaps one or two in a thousand) can become an average or better-than-average speller if he is willing to work on the Spelling List (pages 95–102) for five to fifteen hours, and to follow other reasonable and not-very-time-consuming procedures.

Students who wish to improve their spelling in an efficient way should follow these steps:

1. On a sheet of paper write down in brief form the spelling rules given in section a and refer to them when they are useful. For the word *beginning,* for example, rule 2 will be useful; for *excitable,* rule 4, etc. If you follow this method, you will not have to memorize the rules mechanically, but will learn them in the process of applying them, as a bridge player learns the rules of bidding.

2. Master the Spelling List (section b). When you have learned to spell the words on this list, you will have eliminated half of your spelling errors and will be able to avoid the most glaring and embarrassing blunders. Also you will have developed habits of attention and analysis that will help you in the spelling of words not on the list.

3. Keep a list of words you have misspelled in your writing. Learn this list as you have learned the Spelling List.

4. In revising your writing, look up in the dictionary the spelling of any words you are unsure of. If the word is one you will use frequently, add it to your spelling list.

5. As you read for your college courses, underline new words or terms that are important in your study, and take care to learn their spelling, along with their pronunciation and meaning.

6. Start today to learn the words on the Spelling List and systematically follow the methods suggested as you learn these words and other words.

a. Spelling rules.[1] There are exceptions to nearly all spelling rules, but a sure grasp of a few basic rules will eliminate many common misspellings.

(1) Words spelled with *ie* or *ei* are nearly always spelled correctly according to the old rhyme:

> *I* before *e*
> Except after *c*,
> Or when sounded as *a*,
> As in *neighbor* and *weigh*.

Believe, relief, grieve, chief, piece, niece, field are examples of *i* before *e*. The reversal of the letters when they come after *c* is shown in *receive, deceit, perceive, conceive*. (Some exceptions to the rule are *weird, leisure,* and *seize*.)

(2) Words ending with a consonant double that final consonant before a suffix beginning with a vowel when the word has only one syllable, or is accented on the last syllable, and when the final consonant is preceded by a single vowel:

> begin, beginning, beginner
> stop, stopped, stopping, stoppage
> control, controlled, controlling
> occur, occurring, occurrence

The final consonant is not doubled when it is preceded by a double vowel or two vowels, when the word is not accented on the last syllable, or when the suffix begins with a consonant:

> *Preceded by a double vowel:* need, needed, needing
> *Preceded by two vowels:* treat, treated, treating
> *Word not accented on the last syllable:*
>   offer, offered, offering
>   benefit, benefited, benefiting
> *Suffix beginning with a consonant:* ship, shipped, shipping, [*but*] shipment

(3) Words ending with *y* change the *y* to *i* when a suffix is added, if the *y* is preceded by a consonant:

> lovely, lovelier, loveliest
> mercy, merciful, merciless
> pity, pitiful, pitiless
> copy, copied, copies

An important exception: the *y* is kept before *ing* endings:

> copy, copying
> try, tried, tries, [*but*] trying
> carry, carried, carries, [*but*] carrying

---

[1] Other useful rules are those for the spelling of the possessive case and the plural. See page 5.

The *y* remains *y* when it is preceded by a vowel:
> play, played
> gay, gayer, gayest
> joy, joyous, joyful

Important exceptions are *said, laid, paid* [*not*] sayed, layed, payed.

(4) Words ending in silent *e* drop the *e* when they add a suffix beginning with a vowel, and keep the *e* when they add a suffix beginning with a consonant:

> *Suffix beginning with a vowel:*
> love, loving, lovable
> guide, guiding, guidance
> dine, dining
> become, becoming
> desire, desirable
>
> *Suffix beginning with a consonant:*
> immediate, immediately
> force, forceful
> sincere, sincerely

Exceptions to the rule of dropping the *e* before a vowel are *changeable, noticeable, courageous.* (The *e* is kept to preserve the soft sound of *g* and *c.*) Exceptions to the rule of keeping the *e* before a consonant are *argument, truly, awful.*

(5) The addition of the prefixes *dis-, mis-,* or *un-* does not affect the spelling of the basic word:

> *dis* plus *agree—disagree*
> *mis* plus *spell—misspell*
> *un* plus *necessary—unnecessary*

b. Spelling List: Words and Word-Groups Most Commonly Misspelled. The following scientifically compiled list of words and word-groups is the result of a study of the spelling of college students made by Thomas Clark Pollock,[2] Vice President of New York University. Mr. Pollock examined 31,375 instances of misspelling collected by 599 college teachers in fifty-two colleges and universities in twenty-seven states. Although a total of 4,482 different words were misspelled, Mr. Pollock found that 407 words and word-groups were responsible for fifty percent of the more than thirty thousand instances of misspelling. Thus, by mastering the 407 words or word-groups printed below—a feat that most students can accomplish in less than ten hours—a poor speller can eliminate one half of the errors he now makes in spelling.

The words in the list are grouped on the basis of frequency of misspelling in the 31,375 instances studied; trouble spots in the words are indicated by

---

[2] We are grateful to Mr. Pollock for permission to use the list.

the use of boldface italics, and the number at the right of each word or word-group indicates the frequency with which that particular word was misspelled.

The best way to use this list is to have someone read the words to you and put a checkmark by any word that you misspell or feel uncertain about. One method of learning the checked words is to write them on small slips (with the word *separate,* for example, one would write on one side of the slip the word properly spelled and on the other side *sep—rate* with the trouble spot left blank). The advantage of the slips is that they are easy to carry around and can be referred to in odd moments. Some students, when they have particular trouble with a word, find it helps to work out mnemonic devices—"inf*I*nite is spelled like f*I*nite," "He *ran* with persever*an*ce"—beneath the proper spelling of the word on the slip.

I. Words and Word-Groups Misspelled 100 Times or More

bel*ie*ve		lose		rec*ei*ve	
bel*ie*f	200	losing	184	rec*ei*ving	357
benefit		necessary		referring	140
benefited		unnecessary	103		
beneficial	144			separate	
		occasion	186	separation	216
choose					
chose		occur		similar	109
choice	116	occurred			
		occurring		success	
definite		occurrence	279	succeed	
definitely				succession	140
definition		perform			
define	216	performance	112	than	
				then	125
description		personal			
describe	152	personnel	126	their	
				they're	
environment	126	precede	142	there	440
		principle		too	
exist		principal	123	two	
existence				to	434
existent	305	privilege	127		
				write	
its		professor		writing	
it's	130	profession	104	writer	161

II. Words and Word-Groups Misspelled 50 to 99 Times

acc*omm*o*d*ate	51	contro*ll*ed controlling	99	inte*ll*igence intelligent	65
ach*ie*ve achievement	92	controversy controversial	92	interest	54
acquire	55			interpretation interpret	62
*a*ffect *a*ffective	86	criticism criticize	75	led	64
all right[3]	90	decision decided	50	loneliness lonely	64
among	54	disastrous	56	marriage	57
analyze analysis	87	embarrass	69	Negro Negroes	55
apparent	73	equipped equipment	87	noticeable noticing	58
argument arguing	95	excellent excellence	69	origin original	54
began begin beginner beginning	99	experience	50	passed past	56
busy business	55	explanation	62	possess possession	89
		fascinate	62		
category	71	forty fourth	76	prefer preferred	63
comparative conscience conscientious	50 52	grammar grammatically	68	prejudice	57
conscious	72	height	54	prevalent	66
consistent consistency	67	imagine imaginary imagination	57	probably	58
control		immediate immediately	62	proceed procedure	93

[3] Although the spelling *alright* is also accepted by some dictionaries, it is listed as non-standard usage by others. Many college teachers regard *alright* as a misspelling.

prominent	50	rhythm	84	tries	
psychology				tried	82
psychoanalysis		sense	73		
psychopathic				useful	
psychosomatic	88	shining	50	useless	
				using	59
pursue	50				
		studying	72	varies	
realize				various	72
really	65	surprise	63		
				weather	
repetition	68	thorough	60	whether	81

III. Words and Word-Groups Misspelled 40 to 49 Times

accept		characteristic		hero	
acceptance		characterized	42	heroine	
acceptable				heroic	
accepting	44	coming	45	heroes	45
accident		convenience		humor	
accidentally	42	convenient	46	humorist	
				humorous	43
acquaint		difference			
acquaintance	48	different	45	hypocrisy	
				hypocrite	42
across	40	disappoint	40		
				incident	
aggressive	40	discipline		incidentally	48
		disciple	43		
appear				independent	
appearance	46	dominant		independence	44
		predominant	44		
article	40			liveliest	
		effect	47	livelihood	
athlete				liveliness	
athletic	41	exaggerate	48	lives	41
				mere	46
		foreign			
attended		foreigners	44	operate	42
attendant					
attendance	45	fundamental		opinion	46
		fundamentally	41		
challenge	41			opportunity	45
		government			
character		governor	47	paid	45

SPELLING

p*articular*	44	quan*t*ity	43	sup*p*ose	40
ph*iloso*ph*y*	41	qui*e*t	45	tech*ni*que	44
plan*n*ed	42	re*comm*end	47	transfe*rr*ed	44
pleas*a*nt	42	r*i*dicule r*i*diculous	46	un*usu*al us*ual*ly	41
pos*s*ible	46	spe*e*ch	41		
practic*al*	49	spons*o*r	41	vill*ai*n	45
prepar*e*	47	sum*m*ary sum*m*ed	46	wom*a*n	49

IV. Words and Word-Groups Misspelled 30 to 39 Times

adv*i*ce adv*i*se	30	con*sid*er con*sidera*bl*y*	36	furth*e*r	32
				hap*p*iness	33
appro*a*ch appro*a*ches	31	contin*u*ous	36	hin*dr*ance	31
a*u*thor a*u*thority a*u*tho*ri*tative	36	c*u*ri*o*sity c*u*rious	39	influen*tial* in*flu*ence	30
		depend*e*nt	36	know*l*edge	39
bas*i*s basic*all*y	36	d*e*sir*a*bility d*e*sire	39	labo*r*atory	32
befor*e*	36	effi*ci*ent effi*ci*ency	34	main*t*enance	35
				nin*e*ty	39
car*e*less carefu*l*	35	*e*ntertain	30	op*p*ose op*p*onent	32
carry*ing* carr*ied* carr*ies* carr*ier*	33	extrem*e*ly	36		
		famil*ia*r	37	opt*i*mism par*a*l*l*el	38 35
		fina*ll*y	36	perman*e*nt	38
conc*ei*ve conc*eiva*ble	36	fr*i*endliness fr*i*end	34	permi*t*	35
con*d*em*n*	35	fu*l*fil	34	p*h*y*s*ical	31

piece	34	satire	36	undoubtedly	39
propaganda propagate	32	significance	30	weird	35
		suppress	37		
relieve	38	temperament	34	where	37
religion	38	therefore	32	whose	37
response	33	together	38	you're	38

V. Words and Word-Groups Misspelled 20 to 29 Times

accompanying accompanies accompanied accompaniment	25	attitude	21	divine	24
		boundary	21	especially	27
accomplish	22	Britain Britannica	28	excitable	28
accustom	23	capitalism	24	exercise	29
actually actuality actual	20	certain capital certainly	24	expense	21
				experiment	20
adolescence adolescent	20	chief	24	fallacy	27
		clothes	21	fantasy fantasies	21
against	20	completely	28	favorite	28
amateur	21	counselor counsel council	24	fictitious	24
amount	27				
appreciate appreciation	20			field	20
		curriculum	27	financier financially	27
approximate	27	dealt	28		
		despair	22	forward	23
arouse arousing	22	disease	27	guarantee guaranteed	26
attack	21	divide	28		

SPELLING

gui*d*ance		lux*u*ry	25	*p*hase	25
gui*di*ng	22	mag*a*zine	20	play*wr*ight	25
h*ear*		magnifi*c*ent		politi*ci*an	
h*ere*	25	magnifi*ce*nce	22	politi*ca*l	27
hug*e*	26	man*eu*ver	20	prim*iti*ve	24
hun*g*ry		math*e*matics	26	re*g*ard	24
hun*gri*ly		me*a*nt	27	rel*a*tive	27
hun*ge*r	20	me*ch*anics	20	rem*em*ber	26
ignor*a*nce		med*i*cine		remini*s*ce	28
ignor*a*nt	22	med*i*cal	20		
in*d*ispen*s*able	26	med*ieva*l	21	re*p*re*s*ent	25
int*ell*ect	21	min*ia*ture	20	room*m*ate	24
interfer*e*		misch*ief*	20	sacri*f*ice	21
interf*ere*nce	20	mora*l*		saf*e*ty	23
inter*r*upt	28	moral*e*			
*i*nvolve	29	moral*l*y	25	satis*f*y	
irre*lev*ant	21	narr*a*tive	22	satisf*i*ed	23
lab*o*r*er*		natur*all*y	21	s*c*e*ne*	27
lab*o*ri*o*usly		nob*le*	21	*s*chedule	25
lab*o*r	21	obst*a*cle	22	s*ei*ze	26
lai*d*	26	o*m*it	20	sent*e*nce	23
lat*e*r	21	p*e*ace	21	serge*a*nt	29
l*ei*sure		perc*ei*ve	28	se*v*eral	26
l*ei*surely	29	persist*e*nt	28	she*p*h*er*d	22
len*gth*		p*er*suade	20	sim*p*ly	
leng*the*ning	26			simp*le*	22
li*c*ense	21	p*er*tain	23	sop*h*omore	27
lik*e*ness					
lik*e*ly					
lik*e*lihood	20				

source	25	suspense	28	thought	20
story stories	24	symbol	21	tragedy	20
		synonymous	22	tremendous	23
straight	22	tendency	26		
strength	24	themselves them	22	vacuum	23
strict	21			view	23
substantial	26	theory theories	23	whole	26
subtle	29	those	20	yield	20

c. Spelling Test.[4] The purpose of this test is to let you see how your ability to spell compares with that of a group of other college freshmen. At Tufts University, an entering class of about 700 took this test. The table below records the results:

Rank	Score
Upper 10th	50–46
2nd 10th	45–43
3rd 10th	42–41
4th 10th	40–39
5th 10th	38–37
6th 10th	36
7th 10th	35–34
8th 10th	33–32
9th 10th	31–27
Lowest 10th	26–6

After you have taken the test, check your answers with those supplied at the end of this article, count the number of right answers, and consult the table to see where you stand or sit or lie.

In each of the following lines there will be *either one misspelled word* or *no misspelled word*. If you find a word misspelled, enter the number of the column in which it appears in the blank space to the right of the line; if you find no misspelled word, enter the number 5 (for the appropriate column) in the blank space. DO *NOT* MERELY LEAVE THE BLANK SPACE EMPTY IF THERE IS NO MISSPELLED WORD IN THE LINE.

[4] For this test we are indebted to Harold G. Ridlon, of Tufts University. Professor Ridlon is now chairman of the English Department at Bridgewater State College.

SPELLING

	1	2	3	4	5
(1)	undoubtadly	proceed	equipped	extremely	none _____
(2)	politician	seperate	acquaint	fallacy	none _____
(3)	controversy	sophomore	seize	believe	none _____
(4)	apparent	alright	already	altogether	none _____
(5)	curiosity	similiar	parallel	prominent	none _____
(6)	their	religion	suspense	concievable	none _____
(7)	hinderance	piece	laid	heroes	none _____
(8)	difference	relative	fallacy	sponser	none _____
(9)	disastrous	fourty	accommodate	fulfil	none _____
(10)	benefit	professor	personnel	especially	none _____
(11)	basicly	efficiency	laboratory	opponent	none _____
(12)	environment	analyze	definate	guarantee	none _____
(13)	substantial	influential	grammer	therefore	none _____
(14)	government	exaggerate	height	rhthym	none _____
(15)	wierd	tries	temperament	meant	none _____
(16)	philosophy	indispensible	mathematics	sense	none _____
(17)	definition	approximate	reminicse	completely	none _____
(18)	hypocrisy	acquire	occurrence	achieve	none _____
(19)	theories	catagory	mechanics	necessary	none _____
(20)	tragedy	miniature	prevelant	receive	none _____
(21)	interference	noticable	medicine	maneuver	none _____
(22)	experiment	sacrifice	agressive	adolescence	none _____
(23)	equiptment	affect	ninety	leisurely	none _____
(24)	magazine	desiribility	vacuum	likelihood	none _____
(25)	naturally	capitalism	sentence	transfered	none _____
(26)	lonliness	accompaniment	chief	counselor	none _____
(27)	significance	permanent	optomism	several	none _____
(28)	council	tremendous	despair	consistant	none _____
(29)	criticism	acceptable	begining	challenge	none _____
(30)	morale	accidently	divine	medieval	none _____
(31)	succeed	beneficial	surprise	posession	none _____
(32)	technique	losing	license	persistant	none _____
(33)	occured	fundamentally	comparative	shepherd	none _____
(34)	repetition	explanation	fascinate	humorous	none _____
(35)	primitive	recommend	narrative	fantasies	none _____
(36)	preferred	controling	conscientious	height	none _____
(37)	irrelevant	expense	excellence	villian	none _____
(38)	embarass	immediately	conscious	attendant	none _____
(39)	boundary	pursue	occassion	fictitious	none _____
(40)	marriage	acheivement	grammatically	laborer	none _____
(41)	criticize	independant	perceive	guidance	none _____
(42)	amateur	synonymous	magnificence	interupt	none _____
(43)	quanity	phase	playwright	ignorance	none _____
(44)	forward	roommate	atheletic	pertain	none _____
(45)	discipline	dominant	incidentally	privilege	none _____

104   CAPITALIZATION

	1	2	3	4	5
(46)	surpress	represent	stories	accustom	none ___
(47)	strength	schedule	tendancy	source	none ___
(48)	performance	controlled	benefitted	psychology	none ___
(49)	writing	authoratative	precede	maintenance	none ___
(50)	considerably	financially	existence	arguement	none ___

Answers:

(1) 1	(11) 1	(21) 2	(31) 4	(41) 2
(2) 2	(12) 3	(22) 3	(32) 4	(42) 4
(3) 5	(13) 3	(23) 1	(33) 1	(43) 1
(4) 2	(14) 4	(24) 2	(34) 5	(44) 3
(5) 2	(15) 1	(25) 4	(35) 2	(45) 5
(6) 4	(16) 2	(26) 1	(36) 2	(46) 1
(7) 1	(17) 3	(27) 3	(37) 4	(47) 3
(8) 4	(18) 5	(28) 4	(38) 1	(48) 3
(9) 2	(19) 2	(29) 3	(39) 3	(49) 2
(10) 5	(20) 3	(30) 2	(40) 2	(50) 4

50. CAPITALIZATION   Cap

Although capitalization is not completely standardized, most capitalization is conveniently prescribed by convention. Capitals are used for two general purposes: to mark beginnings and to indicate proper names and words derived from proper names.

a. A capital is used as the initial letter of:

(1) A sentence or group of words punctuated with an end stop.

Will the Senate ratify the measure? Perhaps. If it does, the President will have gained a victory.

(2) A sentence (or sentence equivalent) directly quoted within another sentence.

He said, "You are right."

(3) Traditionally, each line of poetry.

Each might his several province well command,
Would all but stoop to what they understand.

(4) Sometimes a formally introduced series or an independent statement that follows a colon.

A capital is used as an initial letter in: A sentence or group of words that . . . .
A useful spelling rule is: Words ending with *y* change *y* to *i* when a suffix is added, if the *y* is preceded by a consonant.

CAPITALIZATION

b. **One or more capital letters are used for:**

(1) Proper nouns—nouns that name particular persons, places, institutions, organizations, creeds, nations, races, tribes, things (Mary, Fifth Avenue, the Supreme Court, the United Nations, a Baptist, Italy, a Negro, a Mohawk, the Ohio River).

(2) Derivatives of proper nouns (especially adjective derivatives) used with a "proper meaning" (British, Ciceronian, Miltonic). Some derivatives of proper nouns, after long-continued usage, lose their proper meaning and are sometimes written in lower case (venetian blinds, plaster of paris). Good desk dictionaries indicate whether a particular entry is capitalized.

(3) Names of deity and (often) pronouns referring to deity (God, His will, the Holy Spirit).

(4) Names of sacred books or the equivalent of names (Bible, Koran, Old Testament, the Scripture).

(5) Important words in titles of books, periodicals, articles, literary works. It is customary *not* to capitalize an unemphatic article (a, an, the), preposition, or conjunction unless it appears as the first word of the title (*The Turn of the Screw, The Man Who Came to Dinner*).

(6) A title or designation immediately preceding the name of a person (President Nixon, Secretary of State Rogers, Captain Jones, Father Ryan, Chairman Humphrey, Dean Barker). When the title follows the name as an appositive, usage differs. Some authorities would capitalize such appositives only when the titles indicate preeminence or distinction (Richard M. Nixon, President of the United States, or Victoria, Queen of England). In certain contexts, though, less important titles are capitalized. A college newspaper editor might appropriately capitalize: Richard Manifriends, *P*resident of the Student Council, or Mr. Claude Choosey, *D*irector of Admissions.

(7) Many widely used abbreviations for proper names (CORE, WAVE, CARE, UN, N.Y., N.J.).

(8) Academic degrees and their abbreviations (Doctor of Laws, Master of Arts, A. B., Ph.D.).

(9) Days of the week, months of the year, periods of history, holy days and holidays, the abbreviations A.D. and B.C. (Monday, October, the Middle Ages, Good Friday, the Fourth of July, A.D. 307), but *not* autumn or other seasons unless they are personified—"Old Winter with his blustering breath...."

(10) The pronoun *I* and the interjection *O*.

College students ordinarily have little trouble with capitalization. Their only common difficulty comes from failing to distinguish between words used to name a *particular* person, place, or thing (used, that is, as proper nouns), and the same words used in a general way, and therefore not conventionally capitalized. Some illustrations will clarify this distinction.

I told the whole story to Mother. [*Mother* here takes the place of a proper name, and so is capitalized.]

I told the whole story to my mother.

He had an audience with the King. [*King* refers to a particular person.]
He had seen enough of kings and queens. [The words *kings* and *queens* are used generally.]

He went to Elliot High School and then to Oberlin College. [Names of particular institutions]
Since he barely got through high school, he is sure to fail in college.

I used to live on Quincy Street, but now I live on Ashland Boulevard. [Proper names]
They are planning to make this street into a boulevard.

He intends to vote for Mayor Dawson.
Dawson hopes to be elected mayor.

I am taking Mathematics 2 and History 2. [Names of particular courses]
I am taking mathematics and history. [*But*] I am taking French and English. [Names derived from proper nouns]

He comes from the South and does not like the Middle West. [Proper names of sections of the country]
He lives two miles south of town.

EXERCISES

Insert capitals where they are needed in the following sentences.

1. the doctor gave mrs. smith a book entitled *the care of young children* and told her to take it with her on her south american trip.

2. he said that judge black and dr. holmes live on high street near a broad avenue that leads to cherokee park.

3. "the high school i attended was small," mother said. "when i was in college at the university of southern california, i wished i had taken more french and latin; then i could have got my a.b. degree more easily."

4. my father and uncle gerald were freshmen in college together and members of the same fraternity, beta theta pi; later they served together in the united states navy, and both became captains on destroyers before the end of world war ii.

5. mr. martin, my chemistry professor, thinks the republicans are stronger than the democrats in the middle west; professor boyd, who drove west last summer during the months of july and august, says that the negroes and the indians will vote democratic.

51. TITLES

a. Titles of books, magazines, newspapers, and plays are conventionally italicized. This practice should be followed by college students in their writing. Italics are represented in manuscript by underlining.

b. Titles of short pieces—articles, stories, essays, poems, chapters of books—are put in quotation marks. Usage varies on the titles of long poems and essays; usually they are italicized if they are being discussed as separate units, and put in quotation marks if they are regarded as parts of a larger work.

c. Capital letters are used for the first word of a title and for all other words except unemphatic articles, conjunctions, and short prepositions:

>*The Short Stories of Henry James*   *Romeo and Juliet*
>*The Naked and the Dead*   *The Atlantic*
>*How Green Was My Valley*   the New York *Times*

(Note that the name of a city which is part of the title of a newspaper is usually not italicized.)

d. In writing the title of his own theme, the student should center the title on the first line of the first page, and capitalize the first word and all other important words. He should use neither underlining nor quotation marks for this title.

For titles of people see "Capitalization," page 104.

EXERCISES

Correct the writing of titles in the following sentences:

1. His article entitled where is America going? appeared in Saturday review and was later reprinted in reader's digest.
2. He has written three short stories, love lost, the spider, and the quiet around the pool, and one novel, the sadness in the heart.
3. The article Mars in the Columbia encyclopedia enabled me to understand the chapter called the atmosphere of Mars in that difficult book the universe we live in.
4. This week I read the ladies' home journal, the Yale review, time magazine, the Boston herald, and the Sunday New York times, in addition to Shakespeare's Hamlet and Keats' sonnet Bright Star.

52. SYLLABIFICATION   Div

Sometimes, in manuscript as well as in print, it is necessary to divide a word at the end of a line to make a reasonably even margin. Such division is best avoided as much as possible in typed or handwritten manuscript. Where it seems necessary, the following principles should be kept in mind:

a. Words of one syllable are never divided, and words of more than one syllable are divided only between syllables. Often the pronunciation of a word will indicate its syllabification: *re-lief, al-to-geth-er, dis-ad-van-tage.* When pronunciation is not an adequate guide, the dictionary, which shows the syllabification, should be consulted.

b. Words should not be divided in such a way that a single letter stands at the end of one line or the beginning of the next.

c. The hyphen, indicating that the word is divided, is placed at the end of the line, not at the beginning of the next line.

EXERCISES

Which of the following words can properly be divided at the end of a line? How should the division be made?

alone, school, many, obedience, although, through, elegant, enough, height, hilarious, swimming, drowned, interesting, erase, eradicate, irate, italics, heavy, interpretation, difference, additional

53. NUMBERS   Num

a. In formal and informal writing, numbers are usually spelled out when the number can be expressed in one or two words: *two, fifty-three, six hundred, ten thousand, five million.* They are commonly written as figures when more than two words are needed to express them: $29.95; 1,571,142; 10:45 A.M.

b. Figures are used in writing dates, street numbers, page and chapter numbers, and any group of numbers appearing in the same passage.

    May 30, 1964   19 Weston Avenue   Chapter 4, page 215
    Take notes on 3 by 5, 4 by 6, or 5 by 8 cards.

c. Figures are not used, however, in formal invitations and replies.

    Sunday, the twentieth of January, at four o'clock

d. A number is always written out when it occurs at the beginning of a sentence.

Three hundred and sixty people were present.

e. Roman numerals are used for main headings in outlines, usually for chapter headings, for acts and scenes of plays, sometimes for volume numbers in footnotes, and for page numbers in the preliminary pages of books.

A small Roman numeral preceding a larger one is subtracted from it: ix (9), xix (19). The basic Roman numerals from which other numbers are created are: i (1), v (5), x (10), l (50), c (100), d (500), m (1000). The following table shows how these basic numerals are combined to make other numbers:

2	ii	19	xix	70	lxx	200	cc
4	iv	30	xxx	80	lxxx	400	cd
7	vii	38	xxxviii	90	xc	600	dc
9	ix	40	xl	99	xcix	900	cm
12	xii	43	xliii	120	cxx	1500	md
15	xv	51	li	150	cl	2000	mm

EXERCISES

What numbers in the following sentences should be written in words?

1. $5000 is not an adequate income in 1971, however adequate it may have been in the 1st years of the 20th century.
2. I live at 2083 Percy Street; I am 62 years old; I have been unemployed for 1 year, since September 22, 1969; and I have no private income aside from $150.00 from investments. You can reach me by calling 617–2236.
3. *Encyclopaedia Britannica*, I, 863.
4. Mr. John Brown accepts with pleasure the kind invitation of Mr. and Mrs. James Albert Smith for Saturday, June 30, at 3:00.
5. In Chapter 3, page 486, the author says that in 1935 pork chops were 19 cents a pound, lettuce was 5 cents a head, a good suit cost $22.50, and a ton of coal was $10.95.

54. ABBREVIATIONS   Ab

In a time of multiplying national and international organizations, projects, and agencies, space-saving abbreviations appear increasingly in print. SALT (strategic-arms-limitation talks), MIRV (multiple independently targetable reentry vehicles), AFVN (Armed Forces Vietnam), LM (lunar module), FAA (Federal Aviation Administration) are some of many examples. Such abbreviations, especially when they are new, may be confusing; if they become well established, they are convenient short cuts.

In general, students will be wise to avoid in formal and in high informal writing all abbreviations except very well-established ones. If, however, the content of a paper requires frequent repetition of a long name for which there is a recognized abbreviation, it is permissible first to write the full name with the abbreviation following it in parentheses, and after that to use the abbreviation alone: National Institute of Mental Health (NIMH).

a. Well-established abbreviations that are conventional even in formal writing are:

(1) Abbreviations of time accompanying the year or hour: B.C., A.D., a.m., p.m. [or] A.M., P.M.

(2) Certain titles used with proper names: Mr., Mrs., Dr. [but] President Nixon, General Marshall, Governor Ford, Senator Fulbright, Professor Brown, the Honorable James Peel, the Reverend Lloyd Bone.

(3) Titles and degrees used after proper names: Sr., Jr., Ph.D., L.L.D., M.D.

(4) In footnotes, certain conventional abbreviations: *op. cit., ibid.,* cf., p., vol., ed.

(5) A few generally accepted abbreviations for technical terms: T.N.T. (or TNT), D.D.T. (or DDT).

(6) Widely accepted abbreviated names of organizations and government agencies: D.A.R., Y.M.C.A., NBC, NASA, NLRB. (Note that periods, the usual sign of an abbreviation, are omitted in some abbreviated names of organizations, and are generally omitted in names of government agencies.)

b. Other abbreviations should usually be avoided in formal and high informal writing, and especially the following abbreviations:

(1) Abbreviations of countries, states, months, days, streets, and proper names.

(2) Abbreviations of titles, even generally accepted abbreviations like Mr., Mrs., and Dr., when they are not used with proper names.

(3) Slang abbreviations like "lab," "ec," "frat," "phys ed."

EXERCISES

Correct the faulty use of abbreviations in the following sentences:

1. I have an appointment with the Dr. next Tues. at 9:45 a.m.
2. I hope to spend the Xmas vacation, from Dec. 20 to Jan. 3, visiting Rev. Jones & family in Madison, Wis.; his son Jr. is my roommate.

OUTLINE FORM   *111*

    3. Prof. Lane discussed with the ec. class the recent AFL–CIO dispute in Paterson, N.J.
    4. According to an AP report, unemployment in the U.S. has decreased five % since last Feb.
    5. The noted artist Chas. Lee was born in a humble cottage on Elm St. in Springfield, Mass., in the p.m. of November 14, 1920.

55. MANUSCRIPT FORM   Ms

a. A typewritten paper should be double-spaced, on a good grade of standard 8½- by 11-inch paper.

b. A theme in longhand should be written legibly in dark ink, on wide-lined white paper, 8½ by 11 inches.

c. Only one side of the paper should be used.

d. Substantial margins should be left on both sides of each page.

e. The title of the paper should be written, and centered, at the top of the first page.

f. Pages should be numbered with arabic numerals in the upper right-hand corner.

g. The method of endorsement prescribed by the instructor should be carefully followed. The endorsement here recommended is as follows:

    Henry C. Walker [Student's name]
    English 1C [Course and section number]
    October 1, 1971 [Date the paper is due]
    Professor J. S. Holt [Instructor]
    My Brother and I [Title of the paper]

h. The finished paper should be neat and legible; however, slight revisions may be indicated in the following ways:

    (1) The signs, ¶ and "no ¶," in the margin may be used to mark a change in paragraphing.
    (2) The deletion of a word or phrase is indicated by drawing a line through it. Words and phrases to be omitted should *not* be put in parentheses.
    (3) Insertions are written between the lines and indicated by a caret [∧].

56. OUTLINE FORM   Outl

The kind of outline most useful to students in writing informal themes is a rough outline or an informal jotting down and logical grouping of ideas for the paper. The more formal outline usually required for longer papers and sometimes for short ones, is a systematic and conventionalized way of representing the content and organization of a piece of writing. In the formal outline, the headings and subheadings are arranged, and numbered or lettered, in such a way that the order and importance of points in the paper and the relationship between those points is shown exactly and clearly. The formal outline is the skeleton of the paper. However, its very formality and inflexibility sometimes bind the writer to an organization not the best for his material. To avoid being so bound, the writer should begin with a rough outline, and let the formal outline evolve from the material itself. The virtue of the formal outline is that it enables the writer, as well as the reader, to see at a glance the plan and logic of the whole paper.

Outlines usually follow a conventional system of alternating numbers and letters to show the relationships between sections of the material:

    I. _____
        A. _____
        B. _____
        C. _____
            1. _____
            2. _____

    II. _____
        A. _____
            1. _____
            2. _____
                a. _____
                b. _____
            3. _____
        B. _____

    III. _____
        A. _____
            1. _____
            2. _____
            3. _____
        B. _____
        C. _____
            1. _____
            2. _____
                a. _____
                b. _____
                c. _____

    IV. _____
        A. _____

```
        B. _____
            1. _____
            2. _____
                a. _____
                b. _____
        C. _____
        D. _____
```

There are two principal kinds of formal outlines: the *topical outline,* in which the headings are brief phrases or single words; and the more elaborate and less common *sentence outline,* in which the headings are complete sentences. The form adopted should be followed consistently; a complete sentence should not appear unexpectedly in a topical outline, nor should a sentence outline lapse suddenly into phrases or single words in its headings.

Whether the outline is sentence or topical, it should observe three main principles of correct outline form. These three principles are matters not simply of convention and form, but of clear thinking and logical arrangement.

a. Headings and subheadings that are designated by the same kind of number or letter must be of approximately equal importance.

Points I, II, III, and IV must be equally important main divisions of the paper; points A, B, and C under I must be topics of equal weight, all similarly related to I, of which they are subdivisions. (Students should re-examine an outline with more than six major headings. Usually it represents poor division, because the major headings are unequal; some of them could better be made subordinate to a single, more inclusive heading.)

b. Headings of equal importance must be expressed in parallel form. (In the sentence outline, parallel form is maintained as long as each heading is a full sentence.)

This is the familiar principle of parallelism applied to the outline. If A and B are noun phrases, C must be a noun phrase too, since the three of them have the same relationship to I, and a function of the outline is to make such relationships clear.

c. Any heading that has subdivisions must have at least two subdivisions.

This is simply a matter of logic and common sense. A subordinate heading in an outline indicates that a major heading is being divided into parts. Since nothing can be divided into only one part, correct outlines do not have single subheadings.[5]

The outline below violates all three of these principles of good outline form. Its lack of logic may serve to clarify the principles:

---

[5] The one possible exception to this rule is that one may list by itself an example used to develop a particular heading.

MY TASTES IN READING

I. Westerns and detective stories
  A. Excitement and adventure
  B. Relaxation
  C. Quick and easy reading

 II. Biography
  A. Feel that I am learning something

 III. Lytton Strachey's biographies
  A. *Eminent Victorians*
  B. *Queen Victoria*
  C. *Elizabeth and Essex*

 IV. I most enjoy reading actual history
  A. Journals and personal accounts of the war
  B. Books on Russia
  C. Books on American life
    1. *State of the Nation*
    2. *Inside U.S.A.*
    3. *Segregation*

This outline violates the principles of logical outlining in these ways:

(1) The four main headings are not of equal importance. Heading III, "Lytton Strachey's biographies," is not equal to the other headings, but is logically a subdivision of II, "Biography."

(2) The main headings are not expressed in parallel form. I, II, and III are topical in form; IV is a complete sentence.

(3) Heading II has a single subtopic; that is, the topic "Biography" is illogically divided into only one point. Changing III into B under II, and rephrasing A ("Feel that I am learning something") so that A and B are parallel in form would remedy this defect in logic in the outline.

The following formal, topical outline of a student research paper illustrates correct outline form:

THE BATTLE OF TRAFALGAR

I. Situation in 1805
  A. Napoleon's invasion plans
  B. French and Spanish fleet at Cadiz

II. Nelson's command of the English fleet at Cadiz
  A. His plan for victory
    1. Memorandum
    2. Reaction to plan
  B. Condition of his fleet
    1. Smallness of fleet compared to that of enemy
    2. Loss of ships sent to Gibraltar
    3. Request for additional force

III. Preliminaries to attack
   A. October 19
   B. October 20
   C. Dawn of October 21
IV. The advance to attack
   A. Nelson during advance
      1. Presentiment of death
      2. Prayer for victory
      3. His immortal signal
   B. Arrangement of ships in advance
      1. In leeward division
      2. In windward division
V. The battle
   A. Attack of leeward line
      1. Firing on *Royal Sovereign*
      2. Action against *Santa Anna* and *Fougueux*
   B. Attack of windward line
      1. Firing on *Victory*
      2. Attack on *Bucentaure*
      3. Engagement with *Redoubtable*
         a. Damage to French
         b. Injury to Nelson
      4. Other ships in the fighting
   C. English successes in center and rear
      1. *Redoubtable*
      2. *Fougueux*
      3. *Bucentaure*
      4. *Santissima Trinidad*
      5. *Santa Anna*
      6. *Belleisle*'s action against the enemy
   D. Entrance of enemy van
      1. Defeat of two
      2. Flight of three others
      3. Flight of Dumanoir with remainder
VI. Results of battle
   A. Immediate
      1. Death of Nelson
      2. Ships captured by English
   B. Long-run
      1. English superiority on the sea
      2. Cancellation of Napoleon's invasion plans

The sentence outline is more complex than the topical outline: it is longer than a topical outline of the same material, and it often requires more careful phrasing; sometimes there is a certain artificiality and repetition involved in stating points in complete sentences. On the other hand, the sentence outline has the advantage of being more detailed and informative, and so of giving a clearer view of the contents of the paper. The following sentence outline of the same material represented by the topical outline above will illustrate:

THE BATTLE OF TRAFALGAR

I. The situation in 1805 was grave for England.
   A. Napoleon planned to invade England with a large army.
   B. The French and Spanish fleet at Cadiz was to gain temporary control of the Channel for the invasion attempt.
II. Nelson was sent to assume command of the English fleet at Cadiz.
   A. Nelson devised a brilliant plan for victory by a double line of attack.
      1. He described the plan in a memorandum to Collingwood, his second in command.
      2. Commanders and captains received the plan with enthusiasm.
   B. Nelson was seriously concerned about his fleet.
      1. He had only twenty-seven ships of the line compared to the thirty-six the enemy was reported to have.
      2. He was forced to detach a squadron of four to Gibraltar.
      3. He sent the Admiralty an urgent request for additional force.
III. The preliminaries to attack began two days before the battle.
   A. On October 19, the Allies unmoored and the English sailed to the Straits of Gibraltar.
   B. On October 20, the English headed back to Cadiz, discovered the Allies, and trailed them through the night.
   C. At dawn on October 21, the fleets sighted each other, and the Allies headed north to form their battle line.
IV. The advance to attack followed Nelson's plan exactly.
   A. During the advance Nelson remained calm.
      1. He had a calm presentiment of death.
      2. He prayed for victory.
      3. He sent the fleet the signal: "England expects that every man will do his duty."
   B. The English approached in two elongated groups.
      1. Collingwood's *Royal Sovereign* led the leeward division.
      2. Nelson's *Victory* led the windward division.
V. The battle was a decisive victory for the English.
   A. The leeward line attacked the rear.
      1. The *Royal Sovereign* was fired on.
      2. She blasted the *Santa Anna* and the *Fougueux*.
   B. The windward line attacked the center.
      1. The *Victory* was fired on.
      2. She cut line and attacked the *Bucentaure*.
      3. She closed with the *Redoubtable*.
         a. The French were driven from their guns.
         b. Nelson was hit by a French marksman.
      4. Other ships entered the fighting.
   C. The English were victorious in center and rear.

            1. One by one the *Redoubtable,* the *Fougueux,* the *Santissima Trinidad,* and the *Santa Anna* were overcome.
            2. The English ship *Belleisle* raised havoc among the enemy.
        D. The enemy van unsuccessfully entered the action.
            1. Two ships were overcome.
            2. Three others fled to the southeast.
            3. Dumanoir fled with the remainder.
VI. The results of the battle of Trafalgar were important.
    A. The immediate results were these:
        1. Nelson died.
        2. The English captured eighteen ships and broke Allied sea power.
    B. The long-run results were these:
        1. English superiority on the seas was assured.
        2. Napoleon's plan to invade England was cancelled forever.

Formal outlines are correct and useful when they accurately reflect the organization of the paper, and when logical subordination and proper parallelism show the relationship between sections of the material.

HANDBOOK

Section 6

USING THE DICTIONARY

Much of the value of dictionaries is lost by the uninformed use or inadequate use which many people, including some college students, make of these remarkable books. Although students have been, to some extent, familiar with dictionaries for years, they frequently do not know what kinds of information dictionaries contain; and they are frequently incompetent in the most common use of the dictionary—finding the pronunciation or the definition of a word—because they have not familiarized themselves with the methods and symbols by which information is conveyed.

Dictionaries differ, of course, in their size and completeness. The next time the student is in the reference room in the library he should examine such massive unabridged dictionaries as *The Oxford English Dictionary* (ten volumes and supplement); *Webster's Third New International Dictionary of the English Language; The New Standard Dictionary of the English Language; A Dictionary of American English on Historical Principles* (four volumes); and *The Random House Dictionary of the English Language*. Such dictionaries, though invaluable for certain scholarly purposes, are beyond the means of most college students. For ordinary use, a good desk dictionary is entirely satisfactory.

Listed below, in alphabetical order, are six widely-used desk dictionaries:

The American College Dictionary. New York: Random House.
The American Heritage Dictionary of the English Language. Boston: Houghton Mifflin Company.
Funk and Wagnalls Standard College Dictionary, Text Edition. New York: Harcourt, Brace and World.
The Random House Dictionary of the English Language, College Edition. New York: Random House.
Webster's New World Dictionary of the English Language, Second College Edition. Cleveland, Ohio: World Publishing Company.
Webster's Seventh New Collegiate Dictionary. Springfield, Massachusetts: G. and C. Merriam Company.

The way a dictionary presents information about words can best be shown by examining an entry:

fin·ish (fin′ish) *v.t.* **1.** To complete or bring to an end; come to the end of: to *finish* a job; to *finish* a semester. **2.** To use up completely; consume. **3.** To perfect or complete by doing all things requisite or desirable: to *finish* a work of art. **4.** To perfect (a person) in social graces, education, etc. **5.** To give (fabric, wood, etc.) a particular surface quality or effect. **6.** *Informal* To kill, destroy, or defeat. — *v.i.* **7.** To reach or come to an end; stop. — *n.* **1.** The conclusion or last stage of anything; end. **2.** Something that completes or perfects. **3.** Completeness and perfection of detail; smoothness of execution. **4.** Perfection or polish in speech, manners, education, etc. **5.** The surface quality or appearance of textiles, paint, etc.: a rough or glossy *finish.* **6.** Woodwork, such as paneling or doors, used to complete the interior of a building. **7.** A material used in finishing: an oil *finish* on a painting. [< OF *feniss-,* stem of *fenir* to end < L *finire* < *finis* end] — **fin′ish·er** *n.*
— **Syn.** (verb) **1.** conclude, terminate, close. Compare END.

Reprinted by permission from the FUNK & WAGNALLS STANDARD ® COLLEGE DICTIONARY, copyright 1963 by Funk & Wagnalls Company, Inc.

We see that dictionaries give this information about entries: (1) spelling of the word, including the way it is divided into syllables; (2) pronunciation; (3) grammatical function or functions of the word; (4) definitions; (5) etymology or history of the word; (6) sometimes synonyms and antonyms. Dictionaries also supply information about principal parts of irregular verbs, irregular plurals of nouns, case forms of pronouns, capitalization of proper nouns and adjectives derived from proper nouns, idiomatic use of certain words and expressions, and the status of some words and expressions.

The student, to use his dictionary efficiently, should be familiar with the front and back matter; that is, the sections preceding and following the main alphabetical listing of words. He should locate, for easy reference, the table of abbreviations used in the dictionary. Some abbreviations name the grammatical function of a word: *n.* (noun), *v.i.* (intransitive verb); some mark the use of a word in a special field: *Econ.* (Economics), *Geol.* (Geology); some indicate etymology: OF (Old French), Gk. (Greek); still others may be status or stylistic labels: *dial.* (dialectal), *obs.* (obsolete), *illit.* (illiterate), *Brit.* (British rather than American usage). Of particular importance is the section on the plan and use of this dictionary. The owner needs to know, for example, whether to look for biographical names in the general alphabet of the book (as in most dictionaries) or whether to look in a separate listing of biographical names (as in *Webster's Seventh*). Editors of the dictionary describe their policies in arranging several definitions of a word and in giving alternate spellings or pronunciations of a word. Editors also define any restrictive labels they use, such as *colloquial, informal,* or *slang.* Since dictionaries differ somewhat about the meaning of status labels, the owner of a dictionary should be sure that he is interpreting the labels as the editors intended.

In general, the marking of a term as informal, colloquial, dialectal, or slang is not necessarily a condemnation of the term. Though such expressions are out of place in formal writing, the fact that they appear in the dictionary is evidence of their wide use. The writer must judge whether they are appropriate in the context in which he thinks of using them; the dictionary label is not a prohibition but simply an aid to him in judging.

Judgments about usage have been a problem for makers, critics, and users of dictionaries, especially since the publication in 1961 of *Webster's Third New International Dictionary,* on which *Webster's Seventh New Collegiate* is based. In these dictionaries, the Merriam-Webster editors abandoned both the label *colloquial* and the practice of labeling words and phrases that are generally called colloquial. A student using *Webster's Seventh* should be aware that many expressions given without limiting label in that dictionary are marked *colloquial* or *informal* in other dictionaries. The *Standard College Dictionary,* published later, freely uses the label *informal* and also includes full usage notes about a number of troublesome terms. In a recent innovation in dictionary-making, editors of *The American Heritage Dictionary* (1969) submitted some six hundred matters of debatable usage to a panel of more than a hundred experts on language—writers, editors, and public figures who had demonstrated their ability to use English well. Members of this Panel on Usage were by no means unanimous in their judgments; but the Usage Notes following entries in *The American Heritage Dictionary* report the number of panelists who found acceptable or unacceptable the expressions submitted to them. The Usage Notes in this dictionary provide valuable guidance to the student concerned with appropriate usage and style.

In view of disagreements among the panelists of *The American Heritage Dictionary,* it is not surprising that different dictionaries do not always agree about the status of particular words or meanings. For example, *contact* as a verb meaning "to get in touch with" appears without restrictive label or comment in *Webster's Seventh;* it is labeled *informal* and is accompanied by a comment ("This informal usage, regarded with disfavor by some, is widely used") in the *Standard College Dictionary;* and it is found "not appropriate to formal contexts" by sixty-six per cent of *The American Heritage* panel.

USING THE DICTIONARY

When experts do not agree—and even, sometimes, when they do—the writer must rely on his own sense of language. He will develop that sense by reading, listening to, and absorbing the language of educated and able people.

In another way, too, dictionaries cannot take the place of experience with words. Every time a word appears in context it has a meaning at least slightly different from that in other contexts. Dictionary editors note the meaning of the word in a number of contexts and attempt to define it. Sometimes, for further clarification, they distinguish between the meaning of a word and that of other words used as synonyms. For example, here is a part of the entry for the adjective *base* taken from *Webster's New World Dictionary*.

> *SYN.*—**base** implies a putting of one's own interests ahead of one's obligations, as because of greed or cowardice (*base* motives); **mean** suggests a contemptible pettiness of character or conduct (his *mean* attempts to slander her); **ignoble** suggests a lack of high moral or intellectual qualities (to work for an *ignoble* end); **abject**, in careful discrimination, implies debasement and a contemptible lack of self-respect (an *abject* servant); **sordid** connotes the depressing drabness of that which is mean or base (the *sordid* details of their affair); **vile** suggests disgusting foulness or depravity (*vile* epithets); **low** suggests rather generally coarseness, vulgarity, depravity, etc., specifically in reference to taking grossly unfair advantage (so *low* as to kick a cripple's crutch); **degrading** suggests a lowering or corruption of moral standards (the *degrading* aspects of army life). —*ANT.* noble, moral, virtuous.
>
> Page 121
> From *Webster's New World Dictionary, College Edition*, copyright 1964 by The World Publishing Company, Cleveland, Ohio.

The best that dictionary editors can do, though, is to define the central and common meanings of a word; they cannot communicate the full range of meaning and suggestion that the word may take on as it is used in different contexts. For this reason an English instructor may be justified in objecting to the use of a word in a particular context even though that usage appears to be sanctioned by a good dictionary. For this reason, too, it is generally wise not to use a word that one finds in a dictionary (or in word lists) until one has heard or read the word in contexts which further establish the shades of meaning and suggestion that it may carry.

These limitations, however, are slight in comparison with the varied, valuable and interesting information that dictionaries give. Because the dictionary is the most useful of reference books, a student is seriously handicapped unless he has an up-to-date dictionary of his own and knows how to use it well. Knowing and using his dictionary, on the other hand, can greatly increase the student's vocabulary and stimulate new interest in the fascinating study of words.

EXERCISES

1. On a sheet of paper to be turned in to your instructor, supply the following information about the dictionary that you are using in this course.

(a) the full title
(b) the latest copyright date (to be found on the back of the title page)
(c) the pages in the front matter on which the following are discussed: (1) pronunciation, (2) etymologies, (3) synonyms and antonyms, (4) restrictive labels (also called "functional labels," "levels of usage," or "usage labels")

2. Sometimes your dictionary will list alternative pronunciations or spellings. What do the editors say about the standing (i.e., acceptability) of such alternatives?

3. Before consulting your dictionary, pronounce aloud each of the words listed below, then look up each word, consult the pronunciation chart, and pronounce the word carefully in the way or ways indicated in your dictionary. If there are words that you have mispronounced, note beside them on this page the pronunciation or pronunciations given in your dictionary:

abdomen	detour	government	library
athlete	dictionary	hotel	*pièce de résistance*
Beethoven	economics	interesting	Roosevelt
bottle	either	laissez-faire	stomach
chauffeur	farther	leisure	tomato

4. Read the full entry, paying especial attention to etymology, for each of the following words and consider the ways in which word meanings change and develop. Which word seems most interesting to you and why?

agnostic	gerrymander	metaphysics	harrowing
barbecue	glamour	paragraph	sanguine
divine	humor	period	sophomore

(For a full treatment of the history of these words you would find it interesting to consult in the library the *Oxford English Dictionary*.)

5. Choose three words, any three you wish, and look up each in the *Oxford English Dictionary*, *Webster's Dictionary of Synonyms*, and *Roget's Thesaurus*. Consider the usefulness for different purposes of these three books.

6. Choose a common word that you know well and write a dictionary entry for it. Make your entry as complete as you can without consulting a dictionary.

7. Consult your dictionary and jot down the principal parts of the following verbs.

| break | hang (a person) | |
| dive | spring | swim |

8. Below is a list of words similar in appearance and sometimes confused in meaning. Read the list and then look up in your dictionary any words you are not sure about.

adapt, adopt	continual, continuous	peace, piece
all ready, already	credible, credulous	personal, personnel
allusion, illusion	formally, formerly	principal, principle
berth, birth	human, humane	quiet, quite
censor, censure	imply, infer	right, rite
coarse, course	later, latter	stationary, stationery
conscience, conscious	passed, past	weather, whether

9. According to your dictionary, as what parts of speech are the following words used? Are there some uses not appropriate in formal English?

aggravate	enthuse	like
bust	good	slow
contact	human	sure
due (also *due to*)		

10. Examine the following sets of words derived from the same Greek or Latin root. From the words that you know in each list, determine the meaning of the root, and then try to determine the meaning of any unfamiliar words. Look up in the dictionary words about which you are unsure.

1. tele**graph**, phono**graph**, auto**graph**, **graph**ic, **graph**ics, mono**graph**, **graph**ology, dia**gram**, epi**gram**, electrocardio**gram**.
2. con**vert**, di**vert**, per**vert**, re**vert**, sub**vert**, con**vert**ible, extro**vert**, intro**vert**, **vers**e, ad**vers**e, con**vers**ely, ad**vert**isement.
3. **bio**logy, **bio**graphy, **bio**plasm, **bio**genesis, **bio**therapy, **bio**chemistry, anti**bio**tic.
4. **spec**tator, **spec**tacles, in**spec**t, pro**spec**t, a**spec**t, re**spec**t, disre**spec**t, **spec**ter, per**spec**tive, retro**spec**t, intro**spec**tive.
5. **phil**anthropy, **Phil**adelphia, **phil**osophy, Anglo**phile**, biblio**phile**, **phil**harmonic.
6. re**duce**, de**duce**, ad**duce**, se**duce**, pro**duce**, pro**duc**tive, de**duc**tive, in**duc**tion, intro**duce**, e**duc**ate, **duch**ess, **duct**less, aque**duct**.

11. In the lists of words in exercise 10, of how many roots besides the ones in boldface print, and of how many prefixes, can you deduce the meaning? Try to think of other words in which these forms (*tele, phono, epi, mono, con,* etc.) are used.

12. What are the plurals of the following nouns? Consult your dictionary if you are uncertain.

alumnus	deer	index
basis	father-in-law	phenomenon
commander in chief	hanger-on	president-elect
curriculum		

HANDBOOK

Section 7

A GLOSSARY OF USAGE

The purpose of this glossary is to supply information about a number of expressions and constructions in current American usage. As we have suggested elsewhere, accepted usage is not determined by logic or "rules" of grammar, but by the actual prevailing practice of what linguists call the "prestige group," educated people who occupy positions of respect or leadership in their society. Modern grammarians, dictionary makers, and other authorities on language generally agree that their objective is not to *prescribe* what is correct but to *describe* the actual practice of speakers and writers whose use of language determines the standard.

Although these authorities agree that their function is descriptive rather than prescriptive, they are still faced with the difficult problem of giving an accurate description of a language that varies somewhat in different sections, that changes with time, and that is used by about two hundred and fifty million people. It is not surprising, therefore, that dictionaries and books on grammar and usage sometimes differ in their effort to describe the standing of a particular word or expression.

In preparing this glossary we have examined such books as *The Oxford English Dictionary, Webster's Third International Dictionary,* the six desk dictionaries listed in the section on the dictionary, *A Dictionary of American*

Usage by Margaret Nicholson, *The Perrin-Smith Handbook of Current English*, *A Dictionary of Contemporary Usage* by Bergen Evans and Cornelia Evans, *Current American Usage* by Margaret M. Bryant, *Modern American Usage: A Guide* by Wilson Follett (edited and completed by Jacques Barzun and others), H. W. Fowler's *A Dictionary of Modern English Usage* (second edition), and *The Random House Dictionary of the English Language*.

The student, before he uses this glossary, should see "Levels of Usage," p. 63, for a brief discussion of the terms *standard* and *nonstandard, formal, informal,* and *colloquial.*

A, an. *A* is used before words beginning with a consonant sound or a sounded *h*—*a chair, a Yale lock, a house; an* is used before words beginning with a vowel or an unsounded *h*—*an elm, an honor.*

Accept, except. *Accept* is a verb meaning *to receive willingly* or *with approval:* "He accepted the gift"—"He accepted the decision." *Except* may be a verb meaning *to exclude* ("He excepted Tom, but he invited the others"), or it may be a preposition meaning *with the exclusion of:* "Everyone was pleased except the instructor."

Ad. The abbreviated form of *advertisement* is colloquial. The full form is preferable in writing.

Affect, effect. *Affect* is most commonly used as a verb. In one sense it means *to pretend* or *to assume* ("He affected ignorance"); in another sense it means *to influence* or *to move* ("The tragic accident affected him deeply"). Used as a noun, *affect* is a psychological term meaning *feeling* or *emotion*. *Effect* used as a verb means to *bring about* ("to effect the rescue of the trapped miners"); used as a noun, *effect* means *result* or *consequence* ("We were surprised at the effect of his words on his audience").

Aggravate. In formal English *aggravate* means *to make worse* or *more severe*. *Aggravate* in the sense of *to irritate* or *vex* is a colloquial expression appropriate only in very informal writing.

Ain't. A nonstandard contraction of *am not, are not, has not,* and *have not.*

Alibi. In formal usage *alibi* is a noun meaning "the plea or fact that an accused person was elsewhere than at the alleged scene of the offense with which he is charged." The use of *alibi* as a verb or as a vague noun meaning *excuse* or *explanation* is colloquial. "Their *excuse* [rather than *alibi*] was that they had a flat tire."

All right, alright. *All right* is the generally accepted spelling. *Alright* is now regarded as acceptable by some authorities but is labeled nonstandard by others. *The American Heritage Dictionary* calls *alright* "a common misspelling."

All together, altogether. All together means *united. Altogether* means *entirely.*

>The family will be all together this Christmas.
>The injured man was altogether helpless.

Allusion, illusion. An *allusion* is a reference: "The Commencement speaker made several allusions to our college traditions." An *illusion* is a false mental image or impression.

Almost, most. See *Most.*

Altho, tho, thru. These shortened forms of *although, though,* and *through,* despite some objection, are now accepted variant spellings.

Alumnus, alumni, alumna, alumnae. Latin forms kept in English and applied in strict usage to graduates of a school or college; loosely used, however, to refer to former students of a school or college.

>*Alumnus,* masculine singular; *alumni,* masculine plural.
>*Alumna,* feminine singular; *alumnae,* feminine plural.
>*Alumni* is used as a collective term for men and women graduates or former students.

It seems that there are two reasons for keeping the Latin words instead of using the English word *graduate:* (1) the Latin words carry the suggestion of group unity and loyalty to the institution and (2) they enable one to include all past students, whether or not the students are graduates.

Amount, number. Amount refers to mass or quantity—"an amount of money"; *number* refers to countable items—"a number of dollars," "a number of people."

And etc. See *Etc.*

Anyways. Nonstandard for *anyway.*

Anywheres, somewheres. Nonstandard for *anywhere, somewhere.*

As. Frequently used as a connective where *because, for, when, while, since* or some other more exact connective would convey the meaning more clearly.

>I knew that he was there, as I saw him enter the door.
>IMPROVED: I knew that he was there because I saw him enter the door.

As . . . as, so . . . as. In positive comparisons—"Mary is as tall as Helen"—*as . . . as* is the standard usage. In negative comparisons, either *as . . . as* or *so . . . as* is standard usage—"Mary is not so tall as Helen" or "Mary is not as tall as Helen"—and the choice is a matter of taste.

As, that. *As* is not an acceptable substitute for *that* in sentences like: "I don't know *that* [not *as*] he will be able to come."

As to, with respect to. Though these phrases are standard English, they sometimes lead a writer into wordiness or jargon.

> WORDY: He inquired *as to* when I would pay the bill.
> REVISED: He asked *when* . . .
>
> WORDY: She asked a number of questions *with respect to* his absence.
> REVISED: She asked a number of questions *about*. . .

As to (or *as for*) at the beginning of a sentence can serve to emphasize the noun or pronoun that follows: "*As to* [or *as for*] Harry, he was indifferent or unwilling to act."

Awful, awfully. *Awful* in the sense of "inspiring awe" and *awfully* meaning "in a way to inspire awe" are, of course, standard English. *Awful* in the sense of "bad," "ugly," or "disagreeable" is colloquial, and *awfully* in the sense of "very" or "extremely" is also colloquial. *Awful* used as an adverb ("He came awful close to losing") should be avoided in college writing except to represent speech.

Bad, badly. *Bad* is an adjective and *badly* is an adverb. Choice between the two words is usually easy except when a linking verb is used. Linking verbs (*appear, be, seem, become, feel, look, smell, taste, sound,* etc.) are followed by an adjective instead of an adverb, and hence *bad* and not *badly* is established usage in the sentences below.

> He looks bad.
> He feels bad. (The expression *feels badly* occurs frequently in colloquial usage.)
> The apple tastes bad.

Because. See *Reason is because.*

Being as, being that. Misused for *as, because,* or *since.*

> Because it was a hot day the men took off their coats. [Not—*Being as* it was a hot day]

Between, among. In general, *between* is used with two persons or things and *among* with more than two.

> He sat between the two captains.
> He was not among the winners.

But *between* is sometimes used for more than two:

> The voters found it hard to choose between the three candidates.

Broke. *Broke* in the sense of "lacking funds" is colloquial. *Broke* used as the past participle of *break* is nonstandard. "He has *broken* [not *broke*] his arm."

Bunch. In formal English, *bunch* refers to objects that are growing together or fastened together—"a bunch of grapes." Applied to people—"a bunch of sailors"—*bunch* is colloquial usage.

Can. See **May.**

Can't hardly. *Can't hardly* is colloquial for *can hardly* or *can scarcely:* "He can hardly [not *can't hardly*] speak English." *Can't hardly* frequently occurs in speech but is out of place in formal or informal writing.

Can't help but and **cannot help but.** Both of these expressions—"I can't [or cannot] help but be bored by his dull stories"—are established in American usage but are regarded as slovenly by some writers, who prefer "I can't [or cannot] help being bored."

Can't seem. *Can't seem* for *seem unable to*—"I can't seem to do this problem"—occurs in standard conversational English but is out of place in formal or high informal writing.

Case. *Case* is a much overworked word and is responsible for many wordy expressions. Students should not be afraid to use it, but they should avoid it when it is merely padding or when a more exact word is called for.

UNSATISFACTORY: In the case of a word that is difficult to spell, students should consult a dictionary to be sure that they have the correct spelling.
REVISED: To insure correct spelling of difficult words, students should consult the dictionary.

Complected. Although *Webster's Seventh New Collegiate* enters *complected* without restrictive label, other dictionaries describe it as dialectical or colloquial. In formal and high informal English *complexioned* is the accepted expression.

Considerable. Used as an adjective—"He had considerable respect for his employer"—*considerable* is standard English. *Considerable* used as an adverb—"He had considerable [instead of *considerably*] more money than his friend"—is nonstandard English.

Contact. Although *contact* as a verb meaning *get in touch with* is widely used in the language of business and advertising, many people object to it as commercial jargon. The expression is generally out of place in college writing. Sixty-six per cent of the Usage Panel of *The American Heritage Dictionary* found the verb not appropriate to formal contexts.

Contractions. Contractions (*don't, won't, he's, they're,* etc.) are appropriate in conversation and in writing that is personal and informal. In formal, and in most impersonal writing, they are out of place.

Could of. Nonstandard for *could have:* "He could have won." [Not—He *could of* won.]

Couple. Used colloquially in "He ate a couple of oranges." *Couple* in the sense of "married couple" or "young couple" is a usage not limited to colloquial expression.

Data. *Data,* the plural of the Latin *datum,* is used in current English as a collective noun and so may have a singular or a plural verb.

> This data is unconvincing.
> These data are not consistent.

The plural construction is more often used in formal writing.

Definitely. *Definitely* in the sense of *certainly* is a colloquial expression frequently overused by college students.

> Lincoln was *certainly* [in preference to *definitely*] a great president.

Different than. *Different from* ("My book is different from yours") is the more common usage, but *different than* is now regarded as acceptable. *Different to* is British usage.

Disinterested, uninterested. Careful speakers and writers keep the distinction between these two words. *Disinterested* means *impartial, unbiased, objective. Uninterested* means *indifferent, not interested. The American Heritage Dictionary* labels nonstandard the use of *disinterested* to mean *uninterested.*

Don't. *Don't* is properly used as a contraction for *do not:* "I don't, you don't, we don't, they don't." *Don't* used as a contraction for *does not* ("he don't, she don't, it don't") is nonstandard.

Due to. *Due to* in the sense of *because of, owing to,* is avoided by many careful writers. Most authorities on modern usage, however, take the view that though some people object to it, it should be accepted as established usage. *Webster's New World Dictionary* calls the usage colloquial, and says that *due to* is widely used in the sense of *because of* "despite objections by some grammarians."

> Due to the wreck, the train was late. [Debatable usage]
> Because of [or owing to] the wreck, the train was late. [Established formal usage]

Due as an adjective is unquestionably established usage: "The train is due at three o'clock."

Effect. See *Affect.*

Enthuse. This word is described as colloquial or informal in several dictionaries and is entered without restrictive label in *Webster's Seventh New Collegiate.* Although *enthuse* is in wide use, there is objection to it. In college writing it is better to say "He was enthusiastic about [or showed enthusiasm for] the production of *Hamlet*" rather than "He enthused over the production of *Hamlet.*"

Etc. An abbreviation of the Latin *et cetera,* meaning *and so forth. And etc.* is poor usage because the Latin expression already contains the *and. Etc.* is a useful expression when it saves the continued enumeration of the obvious: "Let *A* equal 1, *B* equal 2, *C* equal 3, etc." Sometimes, however, writers use it as a way of avoiding thought. The student who writes, "I came to college to prepare for medical school, to get an education, etc.," has given the reader no definite information by the use of *etc.,* and one suspects that he had nothing definite in mind. It is better to omit *etc.* when the expression is vague or meaningless.

Expect. Expect is colloquial in the sense of *suppose* or *suspect:*

> I expect [suppose] he had reasons for leaving early.
> I expect [suspect] that it was Frank who put the cat in the piano.

Farther, further. In *Current American Usage* Margaret M. Bryant concludes that "the two words are interchangeable in all uses, except that *further* is always used in the sense of 'more' or 'in addition,' as in '. . . as weapons to fight off *further* inquiry' . . . and 'They might be *further* astonished to learn . . . .' "

Fellow. Fellow used in the sense of *young man, boy, suitor* is colloquial usage, and is inappropriate in formal and high informal language.

Fewer, less. In formal English *fewer* refers only to countable things; *less* usually refers to extent, amount, or degree: "If there were fewer children in the neighborhood, there might be less noise."

Field of. The expression *in the field of* is often wordy. "I am majoring in the field of English" is a wordy way of saying "I am majoring in English" or "I am an English major."

Fine. In informal speech *fine* is often a convenient word. It is widely used in the loose sense of *good* or *admirable.* In writing, however, especially in formal writing, it is better to use a more exact word. *Fine* meaning *exact, precise* ("fine distinctions," "fine measurements") is of course appropriate in formal English.

Fix. In the following meanings *fix* is informal or colloquial:

>Repair: He will *fix* the clock.
>Predicament: He was in a peculiar *fix*.
>Arrange: She *fixed* her hair.
>Punish: I will *fix* him for overcharging me.
>Preparing or planning: He was *fixing* to leave early.

Foreign terms. Frequent use of foreign terms in writing or in speech is likely to be regarded as a mark of poor taste and poor manners rather than as a sign of learning. As a general rule it is best to use foreign terms only when there is no English equivalent and when the reader can be expected to understand them.

Get, got. The principal parts of *get* are *get, got, got* or *gotten*. Some people object to the use of *gotten,* but it is clear that both *gotten* and *got* as the past participle are now accepted in American usage.

Get or *got* meaning *to kill,* or *to irritate,* or *to understand,* or *to be obliged to* is colloquial usage, near the level of slang.

Get across as in "to get across an idea" is at best a colloquial expression.

Good, well. *Good* is properly used as an adjective, not an adverb. Expressions in which it is used as an adverb ("He runs good") are at best colloquial. *Well* is an adjective or an adverb.

>The child is good. [*Good* is an adjective.]
>The child is well. [*Well* is an adjective.]
>That apple looks good. [*Good* is an adjective following the linking verb *look.*]
>He runs well. [*Well* is an adverb modifying *runs.*]

Had of. The *of* is superfluous.

>I wish I had [not *had of*] gone.

Had ought, hadn't ought. Inappropriate in written English:

>He *had ought* to go. [*should* or *ought to* go]
>Deborah *hadn't ought* to have done it. [*shouldn't have* or *ought not to have* done it]

Hanged, hung. In formal usage a man is *hanged* and a nonhuman object is *hung:* "He hanged himself with the rope on which his wife had hung the clothes." The principal parts of *hang* in the first sense are *hang, hanged, hanged;* the principal parts of *hang* in the second sense are *hang, hung, hung.* In informal usage, *hang, hung, hung,* is commonly used for any kind of hanging.

Have got. In many uses *got* is superfluous.

FORMAL AND HIGH-LEVEL INFORMAL: I have to be there at five.
COLLOQUIAL: I have got [or, more commonly, I've got] to be there at five.

Healthy, healthful. These two words are now used without fine distinction in informal English. It seems unfortunate, however, to lose the distinction between *healthy*, meaning *in good health*, and *healthful*, meaning *conducive to health*.

Hopefully. *Hopefully* in the sense of *it is to be hoped* or *let us hope* is widely used but is regarded as unacceptable by many authorities. It is better to write *We hope to be home by midnight* rather than "Hopefully, we will be home by midnight."

Human. Human used as a noun ("Humans live longer than dogs") is standard usage. In earlier usage, *human* was an adjective in formal English ("To err is human"), and *human being* was generally used when the noun form was called for.

Imply, infer. To *imply* is to suggest without stating directly; to *infer* is to draw a conclusion, to make an inference, from what someone else has said, or from observed data.

In talking to his daughter the father implied that she was spending too much money. The daughter inferred from her father's words that he would be opposed to her buying a new evening gown.

There has been some tendency in recent years to blur the useful distinction made by these two words, and to use *infer* to mean both *infer* and *imply*. College students should make the distinction.

In back of. *In back of* is informal; in formal English, *behind* is used.
INFORMAL: The tree *in back of* the house....
FORMAL: The tree *behind* the house....

In regard(s) to. *In regards to* is nonstandard for *in regard to*. The expression *in regard to* is often a wordy substitute for *about* or *concerning*.
WORDY: What have you done *in regard to* the shortage of paper?
IMPROVED: What have you done *about* the shortage of paper?

Irregardless. A nonstandard expression meaning *regardless*.
She will go, *regardless* [not *irregardless*] of the weather.

Its, it's. *Its* is the possessive of *it* ("The tree lost *its* leaves") and is spelled without an apostrophe; *it's* is a contraction of *it is* or *it has*.

It's me. Most authorities on present usage regard *It's me* as an acceptable substitute for the formal and often unnatural *It is I* or *It's I*. *It's him* and *It's her*, however, are not acceptable usage.

A GLOSSARY OF USAGE

Kind, this, these. Formal English requires the use of *this kind, that kind, these kinds, those kinds.* The expressions *these kind* ("I like these kind of oranges") and *those kind* ("He buys those kind of shoes") are colloquial and best avoided in writing, even though good writers do occasionally slip into them.

Kind of, sort of. Colloquial for *somewhat* or *rather:* "I am kind of tired today." *Kind of* and *sort of* in this sense are fairly common in speech, but should be avoided in formal or high informal writing.

Lady, woman. Every lady is a woman, but is every woman a lady? *Landlady, Lady* . . . (the wife of a lord), First *Lady* (the wife of the President) are clearly established usages, and the custom of addressing an audience of women as "ladies," or a mixed audience as "ladies and gentlemen," also is well established. A woman in the professions or the arts is referred to as a *woman* (not *lady*) doctor, lawyer, novelist, painter, etc.

The choice between *woman* and *lady* sometimes calls for tact as well as knowledge of usage, but unless there are special considerations, it seems reasonable to use *woman* as the general term for an adult female and to reserve *lady* for special circumstances and connotations. "Mrs. Roosevelt was an admirable *woman* and a charming *lady.*" This principle would suggest the use of *salesgirl* or *saleswoman* rather than *saleslady,* and *cleaning woman* rather than *cleaning lady.*

Lay, lie. *Lay,* a transitive verb meaning *place,* takes an object: "Lay the book on the table." *Lie,* an intransitive verb, does not take an object: "He likes to lie in the sun." The principal parts of *lie* are *lie, lay, lain.* The principal parts of *lay* are *lay, laid, laid.*

Lead, led. The principal parts of the verb *lead* are *lead, led, led.* Note that the past tense is spelled *led:* "He led the man across the street."

Learn, teach. *Learn* in the sense of *to impart knowledge, to teach,* is nonstandard: "I studied with him for a year, but he never *taught* [not *learned*] me anything." The principal parts of *learn* are *learn; learned* or *learnt; learned* or *learnt.*

Leave, let. The verb *leave* in the sense of *let* or *allow* is nonstandard: "*Let* [not *leave*] him go if he wants to."

Lend, loan. In earlier formal English, *lend* was a verb; *loan* was the noun: One *lends* money or one asks for a *loan.* There is considerable authority now for *loan* as a verb, but many careful writers still prefer *lend.* *The College Standard Dictionary* says that *loan* as a verb is standard English, especially business English, in the United States but not in England.

Less. See *Fewer.*

Liable, likely. *Liable* implies exposure or susceptibility to something unpleasant. *Likely* can be used when either favorable or unfavorable consequences are to be expected.

> A child who plays with fire is *liable* to be burned. [*Likely* could also be used here.]
>
> He is *likely* to be his father's heir. [*Liable* would be inappropriate unless being the heir is considered unpleasant.]

Like, as. Although the use of *like* as a substitute for *as* or *as if* is now very common, careful users of English avoid it, especially in formal English.

> Do *as* I do. [Not—Do *like* I do.]
>
> He acted *as if* he wanted to escape. [Not—He acted *like* he wanted to escape.]

The American Heritage Dictionary labels nonstandard the use of *like* as a conjunction in such sentences, and *The Standard College Dictionary* says that in formal American English *like* is not considered acceptable as a conjunction.

Like to, almost. *Like to* in such expressions as "I *liked to* killed myself riding that horse" is a regionalism. In standard English, *almost* or *nearly* should be used.

Line, along the line of. The expression *along the line of* frequently produces wordiness. "Next summer I expect to do work along the line of salesmanship" is a wordy way of saying "I expect to work as a salesman next summer."

Locate, settle. *Locate* is colloquial in the sense of *settle, take up residence.*

> The family *located* [i.e., *settled*] in Iowa.

Loose, lose. *Loose* as an adjective means *unattached;* to *lose* is to *suffer loss.*

> A man with a *loose* belt may *lose* his trousers.

Lots of, a lot of. Colloquial for *many, much, a large amount. A lot* is written as two words.

Mad. Colloquial American usage in the sense of *angry.*

> Dennis knew his family would be *mad* [i.e., *angry*] when they found out he was on probation.

Majority. Properly used in such expressions as: "the majority party," "received a majority of the votes" [i.e., more than half the total], "reached his majority [full legal age] at the age of twenty-one." College students tend to overuse or misuse the word in sentences like:

> The *majority* [*most*] of the campers dislike beans. [*Majority* is a heavy word here.]

A *majority* [*most*] of the lake front has now been sold.

May, can. The important difference between *may* and *can* is that in formal language *may* is used *to request* or *to give permission,* and *can* is used *to express ability to act.*

> May I have this dance?
> Can I find your name in the telephone book?

Mighty. Colloquial as a substitute for *very:* "I am *mighty* [i.e., *very*] sorry I am late."

Most, almost. In colloquial English *most* is sometimes used in the sense of *almost:* "He was ready to drink with *most* [*almost*] anyone." In formal and high informal English, *almost* is the accepted expression.

Muchly. Nonstandard for *much:* "Your *much* [not *muchly*] valued letter arrived today."

Myself. In strict usage *myself* is a reflexive pronoun ("I cut *myself*") or an intensive pronoun ("I *myself* am unable to go, but I shall send a representative"). It is accepted usage to limit *myself* to these two uses in writing. In familiar conversation, however, cultivated people sometimes use *myself* where strict usage would call for *I* or *me:* "The news was quite a shock to Father and Mother and *myself.*"

Nice. In conversation, *nice,* used to indicate general approval, often serves as a convenient expression when a more exact word does not readily come to mind. In writing, when one has time to choose words carefully, more exact words than *nice* are usually preferable. "He is nice" gives less definite information than "He is well mannered" or "He is friendly" or "He is interested in students and easy to talk to." Words like *nice* and *fine* are so general in meaning that they often blur communication.

None. *None* may be either singular or plural.

> None of us is [*or* are] willing to go.

No one. No one is sometimes mistakenly written as a single word, perhaps because it is confused with *none.* It should be written as two words, and it is followed by a singular verb.

Nowhere(s) near. *Nowhere near* is standard English, but *not nearly* is the preferred expression in formal use. *Nowheres near* is nonstandard. "He is *nowhere near* [or *not nearly*] as old as his wife."

Number. See **Amount.**

Of, have. *Of* as a substitute for *have* in such expressions as *could have, would have, might have* is nonstandard usage. "He would *have* [not *of*] come if we had asked him."

Off from, off of. *From* and *of* are superfluous.

>He stepped *off* the platform.

On account of. The use of *on account of* to mean *because* is a regional colloquialism, out of place in standard English. "He was unpopular *because* [not *on account of*] he was stingy."

One. Authorities on usage once insisted that the pronoun *one* should not be followed by *he* or *his* but should be followed by *one*.

>One should choose *one's* [not *his*] words with care.
>When one is asked what *one* [not *he*] thinks, *one* [not *he*] should give an honest answer.

In present-day usage, however, the use of *one . . . he* [or *his*] is in good standing; often the use of *one . . . one* [or *one's*] requires a frequent repetition of *one* and suggests affectation; in such cases it is preferable to use *one . . . he* [or *his*].

Or. When *or* is used to join two or more subjects, the general rule is that the verb is plural if the subjects are plural ("Axes or saws are used to cut the logs") and singular if the subjects are singular ("An axe or a saw is used to cut the logs"). If some of the subjects are plural and some are singular, the verb agrees with the subject nearest it: "A tractor or several horses are used to pull the machine"—"Several horses or a tractor is used to pull the machine."

This last sentence follows the rule, but sounds awkward. It is best to revise such sentences or to rearrange them so that the plural subject is nearest the verb. For a fuller consideration of the use of *or* see "Or" in Margaret Nicholson's *Dictionary of American-English Usage*.

Outside of. Colloquial when used to mean *except for, besides,* or *other than.* "*Except for* [or, colloquial, *outside of*] Gerald, no one in the group knew the words of the song."

Outside of sometimes produces awkward or ambiguous sentences like the following:

>*Outside of* her long nose, her features were good.
>*Outside of* the dirty window, the room looked clean.

Per. Except in technical and commercial writing, *a* or *an* is generally preferable to *per* in such expressions as *per day, per week, per hour.* "His father earned fifteen dollars *a* [rather than *per*] day."

Plenty. *Plenty* used as an adverb meaning *very* (*plenty* cold, *plenty* angry) is colloquial and is often vague in meaning. A reader may wonder whether *plenty tired* means *exhausted,* or *very tired,* or *tired enough to sleep,* or *comfortably tired.*

A GLOSSARY OF USAGE   *137*

Preposition at the end of a sentence. There is no recognized rule of usage that forbids placing a preposition at the end of a sentence; in fact, idiomatic and direct English sometimes requires that the preposition come at the end. Students can concentrate on writing clear, emphatic, rhythmical sentences and can let the prepositions fall where they may.

Principal, principle. These two words are frequently confused. *Principal* is most commonly used as an adjective meaning chief, or first in rank ("the principal difficulty"), or as a noun meaning one who has a chief or leading position ("the principal of the school"—"the principals in the play"). *Principle* means a fundamental truth, law, or rule of conduct ("the principle of relativity"—"a man of principle").

Proposition. Proposition has many meanings. No one questions its use as a more-or-less technical term in mathematics, logic, and grammar, but *Webster's New World Dictionary* labels the following uses as colloquial: an indecent or immoral proposal; a project, business undertaking; a person, problem, undertaking, etc. to be dealt with. In many of its popular uses, *proposition* is a vague word that can well be replaced by a more specific word such as *proposal, plan, scheme, offer, suggestion, project.*

Provided, providing. Both expressions are standard equivalents to *on the condition that; provided* seems to be more frequently used.

I will go *provided* [or *providing*] you go with me.

Often the use of *if* will produce a less heavy sentence: "I will go *if* you will come too."

Quite a. Colloquial usage in such expressions as *quite a few, quite a number, quite a while.* The equivalent expressions *many, a large number, for a long time* are, of course, established usages.

Quote. Quote as a noun for *quotation* or *quotation mark* is informal usage. Eighty-five per cent of the Usage Panel of *The American Heritage Dictionary* found it unacceptable in writing. *Webster's New World Dictionary* marks it colloquial.

Real. In formal and high informal English, *real* used as an adverb in the sense of *very* is not acceptable.

He was very [not *real*] tired.

Reason . . . is because. Margaret M. Bryant (*Current American Usage,* pages 170–171) gives evidence that *the reason . . . is because* is used in formal English, though less frequently than *the reason . . . is that.* College students should know that some people object to *the reason . . . is because,* especially in formal writing, and that there is no similar objection to *the reason . . . is that.* "*The reason* for my failing the course is *that* [or *because*] I spent so much time on my other subjects." Another and shorter way to express the same idea is: "I failed the course because I spent so much time on my other subjects."

Right. Right in the sense of *very*—"That tasted *right* good," "She was *right* tired"—is dialectal or colloquial except in such titles as "The Right Reverend . . ." or "The Right Honorable . . ."

Seem. See *Can't seem.*

Set, sit. *Set* is a transitive verb and so takes an object: "He set the vase on the table." The principal parts of *set* are *set, set, set*. *Sit* is an intransitive verb and so does not take an object: "He often sits before the fire." The principal parts of *sit* are *sit, sat, sat*. An exception to the rule is the use of *set* in reference to fowls and the hatching of eggs, where *set* is used as an intransitive verb: "The hen is setting." Another exception is the use of *set* in "The sun is setting."

Shall, will. In formal usage, many careful writers still try to preserve some of the distinctions between *shall* and *will,* and *should* and *would*. In informal English there is a growing tendency to use *will* in place of the more formal *shall,* and *would* in place of the more formal *should*. For a fuller discussion, see page 31.

Should, would. See page 31.

Should of. *Should of* is sometimes misused for *should have.*

>He should have [not *should of*] answered my letter sooner.

So. Careless or inexperienced writers tend to overuse *so* in joining two independent clauses, and also to use *so* in contexts where *so that* or *and so* is needed to make the meaning immediately clear. *So that* indicates purpose ("He is saving money so that he can marry in the fall"); *and so* indicates result: "He has saved money and so he will be married this fall." The use of *so* as an intensive ("She was so tired" or "She was so angry") is more appropriate in conversation than in writing. Many students can improve their writing by scrutinizing their use of *so* and by substituting a more exact or a more complete expression whenever it is needed. This treatment of *so* is not intended to induce students to avoid the word; it simply recommends discrimination.

Some. In the following sentences *some* is colloquial usage:

>He felt *some* [instead of *somewhat*] better after the game.
>That was *some* [i.e., *an extraordinarily good* or *bad*] fight!

Somewheres. Nonstandard for *somewhere.*

Sort of. See *Kind of.*

Split infinitive. See page 22.

Sure. In formal and high informal usage, *sure* is an adjective and is not properly used as an adverb.

    He surely [not *sure*] knows what he wants.

Swell. Slang in such expressions as *swell party, swell meal.*

Take and. Nonstandard in such expressions as "I'll *take and* write him [I'll write him] a check" or "He *took and* threw [He threw] the television set out the window."

Teach. See *Learn.*

These kind. See *Kind.*

This here, that there. *This here book* or *that there book* is nonstandard for *this book* or *that book.*

Tho. See *Altho.*

Thru. See *Altho.*

Thusly. Not a standard word; use *thus.*

Till, until. There is no difference in factual meaning between the connectives *till* and *until,* and both are established as good usage.

Too, very. Expressions like "He is not too handsome" and "She isn't too eager to go" are slang and are not appropriate in serious writing. Usually in such expressions *very* should be used in the place of *too,* or the expression should be revised to make the meaning more exact.

Try and. Colloquial usage for *try to,* and more appropriate in speech than in writing: "Try and come to see us this weekend" is colloquial for "Try to come to see us this weekend."

Type, type of. In popular speech, expressions like "That *type* [for *type of*] man is dangerous" and "I need a better *type* [for *type of*] paint" are frequently used; in writing, *type of* is the standard expression.

Unique. *The Standard College Dictionary* notes that *unique* is used loosely to mean *unusual, rare,* or *notable.* Since, however, *unique* in formal usage means "being the only one of its kind," it is better to avoid modifying it with words that express degree or intensity. Examples of undesirable usage are *very unique, rather unique,* and *the most unique.* Words like *unusual, rare,* or *remarkable* often are more exact than *unique* in expressing the writer's meaning.

Used to could. Nonstandard for *used to be able to* or *once could.*

>He *used to be able to* [not *used to could*] shoot better than any of us.
>I wish I could swim as well as I *once could* [not *used to could*].

Used to, use to. In writing, *use to* is a nonstandard variant of *used to;* in speech, the two expressions sound the same. "He *used to* [not *use to*] work in the bank."

Want. *Want* for *had better* or *ought* is colloquial: "You want to [had better] come in before it rains." *Want in* and *want out* are, at best, colloquial for *want to come in* and *want to get out.* "Open the door; I *want to come* [not *want*] *in.*"

Way. *Way* for *away* is colloquial: "way over there among the trees" for "away over there among the trees."

Well. See **Good.**

Where . . . at. In sentences like "He doesn't know *where* he is *at,*" the *at* is redundant and should be omitted.

Who, whom. In formal English, *who* is subjective, *whom* objective: "Who is going?" "Whom shall we ask?" Many students of usage now defend the use of *who* in informal English in a sentence like the last one: "Who shall we ask?"

Whose, who's. *Whose* is the possessive form of *who* ("I don't know whose hat that is"); *who's* is a contracted form of *who is* ("I don't know who's coming tonight").

Will, shall. See **Shall, will,** page 138.

-wise. The suffix *wise* occurs in established English words like *otherwise, clockwise,* and *sidewise.* Indiscriminate use of *wise* to form new compounds should, however, be avoided; *moneywise* and *programwise* and *datewise,* for example, are awkward jargon.

You. *You* is often used in speech and in informal writing as an indefinite pronoun in place of *anyone, one, a person,* but such usage is not appropriate in formal writing. In a sentence like "When you are in prison you are sorry that you broke the law" the use of *you* is incongruous; it is advisable to express the idea in another way.

Your, you're. *Your* is the possessive form of *you; you're* is a contraction of *you are:* "You're going to enjoy your English course in college."

HANDBOOK

Section 8

A NOTE ON PLAGIARISM

Plagiarism is the dishonest use of the work of others.

Few students in composition courses plagiarize deliberately; that is, few copy, with conscious dishonesty, another student's theme, or a passage from a book or magazine. But a number of students, feeling the pressure of regular writing assignments and actually confused about the legitimate use of materials, may be tempted to "borrow" sentences and patterns of ideas, or to "get help" on a theme, unless the whole concept of plagiarism is clarified for them. It is the purpose of this note to make clear what plagiarism is and how it can be avoided.

Plagiarism means presenting, *as one's own,* the words, the work, or the opinions of someone else. It is dishonest, since the plagiarist offers as his own, for credit, the language, or information, or thought for which he deserves no credit. It is unintelligent, since it defeats the purpose of the course—improvement of the student's own powers of thinking and communication. It is also dangerous, since penalties for plagiarism are severe; they commonly range from failure on the paper to failure in the course; in some institutions the penalty is dismissal from college.

Plagiarism occurs when one uses the exact language of someone else without putting the quoted material in quotation marks and giving its source. (Exceptions are very well-known quotations, from the Bible or Shakespeare, for example.) In formal papers, the source is acknowledged in a footnote; in informal papers, it may be put in parentheses, or made a part of the text: "Norman Cousins says . . . ." This first type of plagiarism, using without acknowledgment the language of someone else, is easy to understand and to avoid: *when a writer uses the exact words of another writer, or speaker, he must put those words in quotation marks and give their source.*

A second type of plagiarism is more complex. It occurs when the writer presents, as his own, *the sequence of ideas, the arrangement of material, the pattern of thought* of someone else, even though he expresses it in his own words. The language may be his, but he is presenting as the work of his brain, and taking credit for, the work of another's brain. He is, therefore, guilty of plagiarism if he fails to give credit to the original author of the pattern of ideas.

This aspect of plagiarism presents difficulties because the line is sometimes unclear between borrowed thinking and thinking that is our own. We all absorb information and ideas from other people. In this way we learn. But in the normal process of learning, new ideas are digested; they enter our minds and are associated and integrated with ideas already there; when they come out again, their original pattern is broken; they are re-formed and re-arranged. We have made them our own. Plagiarism occurs when a sequence of ideas is transferred from a source to a paper without the process of digestion, integration, and reordering in the writer's mind, and without acknowledgment in the paper.

Students writing informal themes, in which they are usually asked to draw on their own experience and information, can guard against plagiarism by a simple test. They should be able honestly to answer *No* to the following questions:

1. Have I read anything in preparation for writing this paper?
2. Am I deliberately recalling any particular source of information as I write this paper?
3. Am I consulting any source as I write this paper?

If the answer to these questions is *No,* the writer need have no fear of using sources dishonestly. The material in his mind, which he will transfer to his written page, is genuinely digested and his own.

The writing of a research paper presents a somewhat different problem, for here the student is expected to gather material from books and articles read for the purpose of writing the paper. In the careful research paper, however (and this is true of term papers in all college courses), credit is given in footnotes for every idea, conclusion, or piece of information which is not the writer's own; and the writer is careful not to follow closely the wording of the sources he has read. If he wishes to quote, he puts the passage in quotation marks and gives credit to the author in a footnote; but he writes the bulk of the paper in his own words and his own style, using footnotes to acknowledge the facts and ideas he has taken from his reading.

INDEX

a, an, 125
Abbreviations, 109–110
Absolute constructions, 41
Abstract words, 58
accept, except, 125
Active voice, 27
ad, 125
Adjective clause, 41
Adjective phrase, 40
Adjectives, 33–35; after linking verbs, 19–20, 34–35; and adverbs, comparison of, 34; and adverbs, distinguished, 33–35; and adverbs, overuse of, 35; coordinate, 76; descriptive and limiting, 33
Adverbial clause, 41
Adverbial phrase, 40
Adverbs, 33–35; and adjectives, distinguished, 33–35; classes of, 34; comparison of, 34; conjunctive, 34; overuse of, 35
affect, effect, 125
aggravate, 125
Agreement: of pronoun and antecedent, 10–12; of subject and verb, 23–27
ain't, 125
alibi, 125
all right, alright, 125
all together, altogether, 126
allusion, illusion, 126
almost, see *most, almost*, 135
along the line of, see *line*, 134
altho, tho, thru, 126
alumnus, alumni, etc., 126
Ambiguous modifiers, 50
Ambiguous reference of pronouns, 12–13
among, see *between, among*, 127
amount, number, 126
and etc., see *etc.*, 130
Antecedent, and pronoun reference, 10–14
anyways, 126
anywheres, somewheres, 126
Apostrophe, 69–71
Arabic numerals, 109

as (overused), 126
as...as, so...as, 126
as, that, 127
as to, 127
Attitudinal meaning, and conventions, 2–3
away, see *way, away*, 140
awful, awfully, 127

bad, badly, 127
because, see *reason is because*, 137–138
being as, being that, 127
between, among, 127
Bowen, Catherine Drinker, quoted, 47
Brackets, 71
broke, 127–128
bunch, 128

can, see *may*, 135
can't hardly, 128
can't help but, 128
can't seem, 128
Capitalization, 104–106
case (overuse of), 128
Case of pronouns, 8–9
Choice of words, 56–57; see also Words
Clauses: and phrases, distinguished, 40–41; dangling and misplaced, 49–50; defined, 40–41; dependent (or subordinate), 40–41; independent (or main), 41; punctuation between independent, 72–73; used as parts of speech, 41
Coherence: see also Transitions; in sentences, 57–58
Collective nouns, 10, 25–26
Colloquial English, 63
Colon, 71–72
Comma, 72–79; after introductory clause or phrase, 72–74; between independent clauses, 72–73; fault, 45–47, 73; superfluous, 77; to prevent misreading, 77; to set off nonrestrictive modifiers, 74–76
Comparison of adjectives and adverbs, 34

144

Comparisons, illogical, 53–54
complected, 128
Complements, 18–20; defined, 18; faulty, 52; objective, 19, 35; of linking verbs and transitive verbs, 18–20; subjective, 19
Complex sentence, 41
Compound-complex sentence, 41
Compound sentence, 41
Conciseness, see *Economy*
Concreteness, 58
Conjunctions, 37–39; and prepositions, distinguished, 37; coordinating, 37; correlative, 37; exact use of, 38–39; pure, 371; subordinating, 37–37
Conjunctive adverb, 34, 38
Connectives, 36–39; *see also* Conjunctions, Transitions; heavy or incongruous, 39; inexact, 38–39
considerable, 128
Consistency: in pronoun usage, 11–12; in tenses of verbs, 30–31
Constructions, 51–54; absolute, 41; dangling, 48–50; incomplete, illogical, mixed, 53–54
contact, 128
Contractions, 128–129
Contrary-to-fact conditions, 28
Conventions and meaning, 1–3
Coordinating conjunctions, 37
could of, 129
couple, 129

Dangling modifiers, 48–49
Dash, 79–80
data, 129
definitely, 129
Demonstrative pronouns, 7
Dependent clause, 40–41
Descriptive adjectives, 33
Detail, *see* Concreteness, 58
Dickens, Charles, quoted, 44–45
Dictionary, 118–123
different than, 129
disinterested, uninterested, 129
Division of words, 108
don't (usage), 129
due to, 129

Economy, 59
effect, see *affect, effect*, 125
Ellipsis, 80
Elliptical constructions, 49
Emphasis, 59–60

enthuse, 130
etc., 130
except, see *accept, except*, 125
Exclamation point, 80–81
expect, 130
Expression: *see also* Style, Words; imprecise or ineffective, 56–57

farther, further, 130
fellow, 130
fewer, less, 130
field of, 130
Figurative language, 60–61; inappropriate, 61
Figures of speech, 60–61
fine, 130
fix, 131
Focus, and unity in themes, 66–67
Foreign terms, and style, 131
Formal English, 63
Fragmentary sentence, 42–43
Functions of words in sentences, 4–55
further, see *farther, further*, 130
Fused sentences, 45–47

Gerunds, 21–22; possessive with, 6, 22
get, got, 131
Glossary of usage, 124–140
good, well, 131
Grammar: adjectives, 33–36; adverbs, 33–36; clauses, 40–42; conjunctions, 36–40; nouns, 4–7; parts of speech and their functions, 4–55; phrases, 40–42; prepositions, 36–40; pronouns, 7–14; sentence, 42–43, 51–55; types of sentences, 41; verbals (participles, gerunds, infinitives), 20–23; verbs, 15–33

had of, 131
had ought, hadn't ought, 131
hanged, hung, 131
have got, 131–132
healthy, healthful, 132
Historical present tense, 30
hopefully, 132
human, 132
hung, see *hanged, hung*, 131
Hyphen, 81–82

Illogical constructions, 53–54
illusion, see *allusion, illusion*, 126
imply, infer, 132
in back of, 132
in regard(s) to, 132

Incomplete, illogical, and mixed constructions, 53–54
Incomplete sentence, 42–43
Inconsistent pronoun usage, 11–12
Indefinite pronouns, 7–8
Indefinite reference of pronouns, 12–14
Independent clause, 41
Indirect questions, 87
Indirect quotations, 88
infer, see *imply, infer,* 132
Infinitives, 22–23; dangling, 49; split, 22–23
Informal English, 63
Intensive pronoun, 7
Interest, 62–63
Interrogative adverbs, 34
Interrogative pronouns, 7–8
Intransitive verb, 18–19
"*irregardless,*" 132
Italics, 82–83
its, it's, 132
it's me, 132

kind, this, these, 133
kind of, sort of, 133

lady, woman, 133
Language, figurative, 60–61; levels of, 63
lay, lie, 133
lead, led, 133
learn, teach, 133
leave, let, 133
lend, loan, 133
less, see *fewer, less,* 130
Levels of usage, 63
liable, likely, 134
lie, see *lay, lie,* 133
like, as, 134
like to, almost, 134
likely, see *liable, likely,* 134
Limiting adjectives, 33
line (usage), 134
Linking verbs, 18–20
loan, see *lend, loan,* 133
locate, settle, 134
loose, lose, 134
lots of, a lot of, 134

mad, 134
Main clause, 41
majority, 134–135
Manuscript form, 111
may, can, 135
me, see *myself, me,* 135

Meaning, and conventions, 1–3
Metaphor, 61
Metonymy, 61
mighty, 135
Misplaced modifiers, 49–50
Mixed construction, 54
Modifiers, 48–50; ambiguous, 50; dangling, 49; misplaced, 49–50; restrictive and non-restrictive, 74–76; squinting, 50
Monotony in sentences, 67–68
Mood of verbs, 27–28; uses of the subjunctive, 28
most, almost, 135
muchly, 135
myself, me, 135

nice, 135
no one, 135
none, 135
Nonstandard English, 63
Nonrestrictive modifiers, 74–76
not too, see *too,* 139
Nouns: clause, 41; collective, 25–26; function of, 4; phrase, 40; plurals, 5; possessive case, 5–6; proper, 105–106
nowhere(s) near, 135
number, see *amount, number,* 126
Numbers, 108–109

Object: direct and indirect, 18–19; of a preposition, 4, 8
Objective: case, 8; complement, 19, 35
of, have, 135
off from, off of, 136
on account of, 136
one, followed by *he, his,* 136
or, 136
Outline, 111–117; form, 112–114; sentence, illustrated, 115–117; topical, illustrated, 114–115
outside of, 136

Paragraphs, 62
Parallelism, 63–64
Parentheses, 83
Participles, 20–21
Parts of speech, 4–40
Passive voice, 27; weak use of, 27
per, 136
Period, 84–86
Period fault, 42–43, 84
Personal pronouns, 7–9
Personification, 61

Phrases, 40; dangling and misplaced, 49–50
Plagiarism, 141–143
plenty, 136
Plurals, formation of, 5
Pollack, Thomas Clark, Spelling Report, 95 ff.
Porter, Katherine Anne, quoted, 47
Possessive case: of nouns, 5–6; of pronouns, 8
Possessive with the gerund, 6, 22
Predicate, 18
Predicate adjective, predicate nominative, *see* Complements, 19
Prepositions, 36–37; and conjunctions, distinguished, 37; idiomatic use of, 36–37; use at end of sentence, 37, 137
principal, principle, 137
Principal parts of verbs, 15–18; common verbs, 16–18
Pronouns, 7–14; agreement with antecedent, 10–12; case, 8; classes of, 7–8; functions of, 7; reference, 12–14
Proper nouns, 105–106
proposition, 137
provided, providing, 137
Punctuation, 42–48, 69–91; apostrophe, 69–71; brackets, 71; colon, 71–72; comma, 72–79; dash, 79–80; ellipsis, 80; exclamation point, 80–81; fragmentary sentence, 42–45; hyphen, 81–82; italics, 82–83; parentheses, 83; period, 84–86; question mark, 86–87; quotation marks, 87–90; restrictive and nonrestrictive modifiers, 74–76; run-together sentence, 45–48; semicolon, 90–91

Question mark, 86–87
Questions, indirect, 87
quite a, 137
Quotation marks, 87–90; with other marks of punctuation, 88–90
Quotations, indirect, 88
quote, 137

real, for *very*, 137
reason is because, 137–138
Reference of pronouns, 12–14
Reflexive pronoun, 7
Regular and irregular verbs, 15
Relative pronouns, 7–8
Repetition, 64
Restrictive and nonrestrictive modifiers, 74–76
Ridlon, Harold C., spelling test, 102–104

right, 138
Roman numerals, 109
Run-together sentence, 45–48

seem, see *can't seem*, 128
Semicolon, 90–91
Sentence connector, *see* Conjunctive adverb, 34, 38
Sentence outline, 115–117
Sentences: complete, incomplete, and fragmentary, 42–43; defined, 42; faulty relationships of elements of, 51–55; fragmentary, 42–43; functions of words in, 4 ff.; fused, 45–47; incomplete, 43; run-together, 45–47; simple, complex, compound, and compound-complex, 41; unity in, 66–67
set, sit, 138
settle, see *locate, settle*, 134
shall and *will*, 31–32, 138
should and *would*, 31–32
should of, 138
Simile, 61
Simple sentence, 41
sit, set, 138
so (usage), 138
so . . . as, see *as . . . as, so . . . as*, 126
some, 138
somewheres, 138
sort of, see *kind of, sort of*, 133
Speech, figures of, defined, 60–61
Spelling, 92–104; lists of commonly misspelled words, 96–102; Pollack report on, 95 ff.; rules, 94–95; test, 102–104
Split infinitive, 22–23
Standard College Dictionary, The, quoted, 119
Standard English, 63
Steinbeck, John, quoted, 47
Style, 56–68; *see also* Meaning, Sentences, Words; heavy or incongruous connectives, 39; overuse of adjectives and adverbs, 35
Subjective complement, 19, 34–35
Subjunctive mood, uses of, 28
Subordinate clause, 40–41
Subordinating conjunctions, 37–38
Subordination, 64–65
sure, 139
swell, 139
Syllabification, 108

take and, 139
teach, see *learn, teach*, 133

Tense of verbs, 29–33
that there, see *this here*, 139
these kind, see *kind, this, these*, 133
this here, 139
tho, see *altho*, 126
thru, see *altho*, 126
thusly, 139
till, until, 139
Title, form of, 107
Tone, 65–66
too, for *very*, 139
Topic outline, 114–115
Transitions, 66
Transitive verb, 18–19
try and, 139
type, type of, 139

Underlining, *see* Italics, 82–83
unique, 139
Unity, and focus, 66–67
until, see *till, until*, 139
Usage: and the dictionary, 120–121; glossary of, 124–140; grammatical, 4–40 (of adjectives and adverbs, 33–36; of nouns, 4–7; of prepositions and conjunctions, 36–40; of pronouns, 7–14; of verbs, 15–33); varieties of, 63
used to, use to, 140
used to could, 140

Vagueness, *see* Concreteness, 58
Variety, 67–68

Verbals, 20–23
Verbs, 15–33; + adverb combinations, 19–20; agreement, 23–27; and complements, 18–20; and verbals, distinguished, 20–21; linking, 18–20; mood, 27–28; principal parts, 15–18; regular and irregular, 15; tense, 29–33; transitive and intransitive, 18–19; uses of the subjunctive, 28; verb phrase, 40; voice, 27
Vocabulary: see also *Words*; glossary of usage, 124–140

want (usage), 140
way, away, 140
Weak passive, 27
Webster's New World Dictionary, quoted, 121
well, see *good, well*, 131
where . . . at, 140
who, whom, 140
whose, who's, 140
will and *shall*, see *shall* and *will*, 138
-wise, 140
woman, see *lady, woman*, 133
Words: *see also* Style; and the use of the dictionary, 118–123; choice of, 56–57; concrete, 58; division of, 108; glossary of usage, 124–140; repetition, 64
would and *should*, see *should* and *would*, 31

you, 140; indefinite use of, 13–14
your, you're, 140

CORRECTION SYMBOLS

Ab	Undesirable abbreviation. 109–111.	Div	Incorrect division of words. 108.
Abst	Abstract. Substitute concrete expression. 58.	DM	Dangling or misplaced modifier. 48–51
Adj	See adjectives and adverbs. 33–36.	Econ	Lack of economy. 59.
Adv	See adjectives and adverbs. 33–36.	Emph	Poor emphasis. Improve. 59–60.
Agr	Faulty agreement: of subject and verb, 23–27; of pronoun and antecedent, 10–12.	Exp	Poor expression. Rephrase. 56–57.
Apos	Apostrophe needed or misused. 69–71.	Fig	Trite or inappropriate figure of speech 60–61.
Awk	Awkwardly phrased. Improve expression.	Focus	Weak in focus or unity. 66–67.
Begin	Poor opening paragraph. 62.	Fog	Foggy thinking, or foggy expression, or both. Clarify.
C	Comma needed or misused. 72–79.	Frag	Fragmentary sentence. 42–45.
Cap	Error in the use of capital letters. 104–106.	Fused	Fused sentence. 45–48.
CF	Comma fault. 45–48.	Gl	See this expression in the Glossary 124–140.
Ch	Poor choice of expression. 56–57.	Gr	Obvious error in grammar. Correct.
Choppy	Short, choppy sentences.	H	Hyphen. 81–82.
Cl	Not clear. Rephrase.	Heavy	Heavy expression. 63.
Coh	Not coherent. Make the relationship between the ideas clear. 57–58.	Id	Idiom; unidiomatic usage.
Con	Poor choice of connective. 36–40.	Int	Lacking in interest. 62–63.
Conj	Conjunction. 36–40.	Ital	Underline to indicate italics. 82–83.
Cons	Lack of consistency; undesirable shift.	K	Awkwardly phrased. Improve expression.
Cst	Faulty construction. 51–55.	Lev	Inappropriate level of usage or variety of English. 63.
D	Delete.	Log	Lack of logic.
Dash	Dash needed or misused. 79–80.	Mod	Dangling or misplaced modifier. 48–51.
Def	Definition needed, or unsatisfactory definition.	Monot	Monotonous sentence structure. 67–68.
Devel	Poor development or inadequate development of the idea. 62.		

Below is a list of symbols and abbreviations frequently used by instructors in correcting papers. The numbers following the entries refer to the pages in this book on which the error or weakness is discussed.

Ms	Incorrect manuscript form. 111.
No ¶	Undesirable paragraph break.
¶	New paragraph needed, or paragraphing unsatisfactory. 62.
Num	Incorrect writing of numbers. 108–109.
Outl	Faulty outline form. 111–117.
P	Error in punctuation. 69–91.
Pad	Padding. Strike out unnecessary words. 59.
Par	Faulty parallelism. 63–64.
‖	Faulty parallelism. 63–64.
Pass	Weak passive. Change to active. 27.
Pattern	Undesirable repetition of the same sentence pattern. 64.
PF	Period fault. 42–45.
Poor ¶	Poor paragraph. 62.
Prin	Principal parts of verbs. 15–18.
Pron	Pronoun misused. 7–14.
Quot	Quotation marks needed or misused. 87–90.
Ref	Faulty reference of pronouns. 12–14.
Rep	Awkward repetition of sounds, words, ideas, or sentence patterns. 64.
Rest	Error in punctuating restrictive or non-restrictive modifiers. 74–76.
Run	Unsatisfactory run-together sentences. 45–48.
Semi	Semicolon needed or misused. 90–91.
Shift	Inconsistency, undesirable shift.
Sp	Error in spelling. 92–104.
Sub	Lack of subordination or poor subordination. 64–65.
Tense	Error in tense of verbs. 29–33.
Thin	Lacking substance.
Tone	Inappropriate tone. 65–66.
Trans	Lack of transition. 66.
Trite	Trite expression. 61.
Und	Underline to indicate italics. 82–83.
Unity	Lack of unity. 66–67.
Usage	Incorrect or questionable usage. See this expression in the Glossary. 124–140.
Var	Lack of variety in sentence structure. 67–68.
Verb	Error in verb usage. 15–33.
Wordy	Wordiness: padding, jargon, weak clauses, wordy phrasing. 59.
WO	Awkward or unclear word order. Rearrange.
WW	Wrong word or expression. 56–57.
∧	Omission of material.
X	Careless error.

Additional Correction Symbols: